Explore the Power of Astrology

# Trikona
## Two

*An advanced approach to three
important houses of the chart*

**Dr. Ambika Prasad Parashar
Dr. Vinod Kumar Parashar**

**UNICORN BOOKS**

*Publishers*
**UNICORN BOOKS,** New Delhi-110002

*E-mail:* unicornbooks@vsnl.com
*Website:* www.unicornbooks.in • www.kidscorner.in

*Distributors*
**Pustak Mahal,** Delhi
J-3/16 , Daryaganj, New Delhi-110002
☎ 23276539, 23272783, 23272784 • *Fax:* 011-23260518
*E-mail:* info@pustakmahal.com
*Website:* www.pustakmahal.com

*London Office*
51, Severn Crescents, Slough, Berkshire, SL 38 UU, England
*E-mail:* pustakmahaluk@pustakmahal.com

*Sales Centre*
10-B, Netaji Subhash Marg, Daryaganj, New Delhi-110002
☎ 23268292, 23268293, 23279900 • *Fax:* 011-23280567
*E-mail:* rapidexdelhi@indiatimes.com

*Branch Offices*
**Bangalore:** ☎ 22234025
*E-mail:* pmblr@sancharnet.in • pustak@sancharnet.in
**Mumbai:** ☎ 22010941
*E-mail:* rapidex@bom5.vsnl.net.in
**Patna:** ☎ 3294193 • *Telefax:* 0612-2302719
*E-mail:* rapidexptn@rediffmail.com
**Hyderabad:** *Telefax:* 040-24737290
*E-mail:* pustakmahalhyd@yahoo.co.in

*Printed at :* Param Offsetters, Okhla, New Delhi-110020

# Acknowledgement

The author thankfully acknowledges the help and facilities provided by Sanjaya Parashar, the youngest son, while completing this work. The author feels thankful to the members of his family, especially his eldest son, Suresh Chandra Parashar, who directly or indirectly inspired him to write this book. He also feels happy that his second son, Dr. V.K. Parashar, joined him in completing this project. He also gratefully acknowledges the help provided by the Brazoria County Library, Angleton, in Texas, USA, that enabled him to complete this uncommon project on astrology. The author is highly thankful to the writers, both in India and abroad, who with their hard work and intuition have provided immense informative material that has helped him to analyse and summarise the findings relating to astrological material presented in this book. The author is also thankful to Dr. Ashok Gupta, MD, Unicorn Books, for accepting this work and making it available to all those who are interested to know more about these three important angles in a chart.

APP

VKP

e-mail: ap_98607@yahoo.co.in

*by the same authors*

- Explore the Power of Astrology
- Explore the Power of Astrology—Trikona 1


*by Dr. A.P. Sharma*

- Thorn in My Rose Bush
- Sentence Correction for Admission to Foreign Universities
- Words & Phrases that carry Uncommon Meanings
- The Meaning to Know Thyself
- From Despair to Joy

# Contents

*Chapter One :* **I Need Your Attention**   7

On Studying Astrology ................................................................7

Dimensions of Trikona Two ........................................................9

Understanding the Planets ........................................................ 11


*Chapter Two :* **The Third House**   15

*House of Communication, Journeys,*
*Brothers & Sisters*

Transits of Planets ..................................................................... 17

Analysis of the Charts .............................................................. 29

Brief Summary of Results .......................................................... 48


*Chapter Three :* **The Seventh House**   50

*House of Romance, Marriage & Legal Affairs*

Transits of Planets ..................................................................... 51

Analysis of the Charts .............................................................. 61

Brief Summary of Results .......................................................... 84

When Matching Charts for Marriage! ....................................... 85


*Chapter Four :* **The Eleventh House**   88

*House of Idealism, Dreams and Riches*

Transits of Planets ..................................................................... 89

Analysis of the Charts .............................................................. 100

The Concluding Chart ............................................................. 121

Specific Discussions.................................................................. 122

Brief Summary of Results .......................................................... 124

## APPENDICES

*Appendix-I* : The Zodiac Signs   129

*Appendix-II* : The Houses   142

*Appendix-III* : Different Aspects from
Different Positions   149

*Appendix-IV* : Retrograding Planets   151

# I Need Your Attention

## On Studying Astrology

𝒜strology studies the movements of the planets and their influence on human beings on the earth. Most of us who love to study astrology incline to learn it as a system that uses the outer world as a symbol for the inner world. In fact, if you are really interested, you must not abide by any kind of prejudices, for they will not permit you to understand what it is. If you sincerely study it with an open mind and curiosity, you can easily know how stars influence human beings and world events.

There are many people who don't care to know what astrology is or how it can enlighten humans in different areas of life. But there are a great number of people who do believe that astrology can do wonders and can help solve different kinds of human problems. They also hold that it can show them some way to reach their goals successfully. Well, whether astrology really works is an important question. The astrologers of the olden times had a maxim that they unfolded boldly in their books on this subject: "The stars incline, they do not compel." In other words, under the influence of the planets, you may feel tired but that planetary influence cannot force you to fly or to drive a car or make you feel hungry when you have a stomach disorder.

In fact, traditional Indian astrology is quite complex as well as different in many ways from Western astrology. One of the main differences is the dates of the Sun's transits from one sign to the other sign. According to Indian astrological traditions, the Sun normally transits a sign around the 13th or 14th day of a month and stays in that sign for almost one month. Western astrologers reckon that the Sun transits from one sign to another around the 22nd day of a month and stays there for one month. For example, the Sun enters in Aries on 14th April according to the Indian astrological tradition, whereas Western astrologers consider the Sun's entry in Aries to be around 22nd March. Both the systems also differ in identifying certain characteristics that are aligned to the Sun signs in different symbols. Without getting confused by mingling the two systems, the reader is advised to follow one system only, preferably the Indian system, not because we feel identified with it, but because the Indian traditions relating to astrological knowledge are much more accurate and comparatively older than the Western astrological traditions.

In order to know more about the future of a human being it is imperative to cast a birth-chart (*kundali*) of a person at the time of his/her birth. How to make that chart has been fully explained in our first book, **Explore the Power of Astrology**. You need to know one's exact time and place of birth to make a correct chart (*kundali*) which may help you to predict events of one's life correctly (2: p.xxii). You may be quite familiar with the Sun signs but they are just the beginning of the process. All the twelve signs appear somewhere in your own birth-chart and in addition to the Sun, the Moon, Jupiter, Mercury, Venus and other planets also appear in the chart somewhere. Based on the date, place and time of your birth, the signs in the houses create your astrological birth-chart (*kundali*), which tells more about yourself and about your life. In fact, it can tell all about you, your personality, your likes and dislikes, your inclinations, your love life, your married life, your children, your spouse, your creativity, job opportunities, the areas of jobs where you will succeed better, your finances, the number and position of your sisters and brothers, and your social status as well.

## Dimensions of Trikona Two

Truly speaking, practically there is no area of life to which astrology cannot be usefully applied—starting from one's birth right through to one's retirement. It would not be true to state that wherever human life is, so also is astrology. As you go through this book you will gradually be more convinced of that. Since we are concentrating on a set of three angles or houses in this book, we will primarily deal with matters relating to those three houses or angles only. These are **the third house, the seventh house** and **the eleventh house.** The reader may get confused as to which is the third or the eleventh house in a chart. Traditionally, Indian astrologers count the houses in anti-clockwise manner. Therefore, the house which is counted as the third from the ascendant is the third house whereas the house counted as the eleventh from the ascendant is considered to be the eleventh house.

*The third house* is known as the house of brothers, friends, general education, short travels and personal efforts; *the seventh house* is known as the house of partner, and partnership in business, the house that also indicates the time of death and time of marriage etc.; *the eleventh house* is known as the house of social status, opportunities regarding money earned through the stroke of luck, and one's total riches in life. **Surprisingly, like the first three important houses (the first house, fifth house and the ninth house) that can predict most of your life's big and important events, these three houses can also predict the other important areas of your life. Hence they are equally important astrologically.**

Although elaborate explanations have been presented by us on all the twelve houses in our first book, **Explore the Power of Astrology,** this book, i.e. **Trikona *Two,*** like **Trikona *One,*** is an advanced approach to the three very vital houses, which unfold much more than what we normally know about them. Hence a detailed treatment is given to them in **Trikona** *Two* for the benefit of the interested reader. It is hoped that like our first two books on astrology, **Trikona** *Two* will also be appreciated by you. If our humble attempt inspires you, and you believe that you have learnt more about astrology after reading **Trikona** *Two*, we shall feel rewarded. A good number of charts (*kundalis*) have been analysed in all the three related areas in **Trikona** *Two* to help the reader understand various planetary combinations, planets' aspects and different *yogas* that they form when they sit with the other planets in a house.

In fact, there is specific meaning to which houses your planets are in. It is one more step in unlocking the mystery of you. Any house in your birth-chart with more than one planet in it shows an area of your life that is strengthened and emphasised. At the same time houses without any planets are also active. It all depends on the ruler of the house and the aspects on the house. A house without any planet in it can be just as strong as one with the planets. The house ruler describes what is happening in the area of your life. Please keep in mind that all houses have rulers and landlords that are ultimately in charge of the house. A planet in a house can be known as a 'resident landlord.' It affects one's life in that area.

In order to provide you specific knowledge of a house, its landlord and various aspects of the planets on a house, we have presented a good number of birth-charts at the end of each chapter that relates to the three specific houses—*third house, seventh house* and *eleventh house*. But before we begin our discussions on **Trikona** *Two*, we would like the reader to go through briefly once again the **12 zodiac signs** to which certain major qualities are associated. It is absolutely important to revise it at this juncture for it may help you understand the influence of the Sun on one's life. For your immediate reference, a brief description of the twelve zodiac signs is given at the conclusion of this book in Appendix 1.

In fact, the Sun is the most powerful planet astrologically. When the Sun transits different zodiac signs, it governs different characteristics which it bestows upon the individual accordingly. Therefore, the position of the Sun in a birth-chart governs one's individuality, distinctive style and the drives that fulfil one's goals to a large extent. As the artist may outline your general shape including the planes, the angles of your face, the way in which you hold your body, in the same manner the Sun signs determine your general character. How do you deal with your responsibility? Are you an easygoing person or persistently follow your life's goals? Answers of many of these questions may be found to a great extent in your Sun sign given in detail in Chapter One of our first book, **Explore the Power of Astrology.**

Before I wind up this small informative section of the book, I humbly beseech the reader to go through the basic qualities associated with each planet so that predictions relating to those planets will be easily conceived in your mind. If the basic characteristics of the planets are understood well, it will provide you an insight with which you can easily unfold the hidden and overt impact of a planet(s) placed in a house as well as through its aspects or placement or ownership.

## Understanding the Planets

It is primarily your intuition that can help you understand and interpret any chart (*kundali*) and provide you clarity. It is the indispensable connection between your intuition, manifold influences of the planets and the secrets of astrology that unfold the hidden secrets into a coherent whole making it a living history. Without your intuition you would simply read the symbols and there will only be a broad knowledge of the planets and no real understanding.

Planets are classified as benefic or malefic—good or bad, but unless we try to know them intimately, we would not know them well. Let us briefly discuss their qualities.

*The Sun is conceived* as the essence and energy of life, manifestation of will power and drive. It also represents the ego, individuality and principles of life. It provides us the thrust that allows us to meet the challenges and help to expand our lives. It also represents creativity. It also indicates the general state of our physical health. It symbolises the natural father in the chart. It indicates how much authority, leadership and power an individual possesses. Thus, the Sun represents the basic qualities which makes a man spirited, powerful and full of leadership ability.

*The Moon is related* to the mother, your inner self, and all the activities that are related to your feelings, emotions and passions. It represents professions dealing with children and the sea. Astrologers also connect it with professions related with jewellery, especially pearls, glass and white stone. It represents your moods, impulsiveness and sensuous feelings that are related to your mate. The Moon also discloses the quality and working of your heart and provides the overall inner activities hooked with your mind.

*Mars is related* to your dynamic expressions. It is connected to your aggressive nature and individualism. It also indicates your sex drives and your actions. Mars dictates your survival energy. It refuses to compromise as it has its own way of thinking and reacting because it has its own individuality. Mars loves freedom but no domination. It also doesn't like to indulge in denials, but being of independent nature it always prefers to remain free. Mars is always connected with war and therefore aggressive disposition is quite natural with the people dominated by Mars.

*Mercury indicates* intellectual abilities, mental quickness and alertness, verbal activity, communication. It represents your mental picture of the world you see. Mercury indicates logical power and reasoning abilities. It represents how we think and how we communicate the conceived thoughts. It is also connected with your routine travelling, just simple trips across the town and not long distance tours. It represents your writing capability and power of expression, both verbal and written. It deals with teaching, speaking, books, publication, and rules arms, hands, shoulders, lungs, nervous and respiratory systems.

*Jupiter is linked* with your luck. It relates to your higher mind that deals with your religious and philosophical ideals. It is related with higher education, your expansion in life, integration and growth. It is associated with luck, success, achievement and prosperity. It bestows love for travelling and inspires you to discover that there is need to explore philosophical and religious ideas and integrate them into the larger social order indicative of religious institutions like temple, church and any such others. Above all, Jupiter rules our abstract mind and describes our intellectual and spiritual interests in the most profound and intimate manner. A badly placed Jupiter indicates laziness and inactive disposition in a native.

*Venus represents* romance, beauty and artistic instincts and sociability. It also indicates how much ability you possess to attract compatible people and to create close and intimate relationships with them. It indicates your personal qualities that help you in forming business partnerships. Venus is also associated with arts, and the aesthetic sense you possess. It is considered to exert great influence on your instincts relating to music, art and literature. Since it is directly related to your romantic feelings, it is connected with your spouse and thoughts connected to him/her.

*Saturn is related* to discipline, your responsibility and limitations. It represents restrictions and obedience, with no free rides for you. It provides structure and foundation which help you grow pragmatically in your life. It is your practical self through which you learn the rules of the game regarding physical reality. If Saturn is well placed in a chart it leads you to be prudent, possessing a practical outlook in life.

**Rahu & Ketu possess** the qualities of the sign they occupy. They don't have their own qualities. They feel at home when they occupy the signs ruled by Venus and Mercury and are quite happy in the signs ruled by Saturn. When they transit in other signs they may indicate some of their qualities but with a difference, in the sense that they certainly lead the individual to think and act negatively to a certain extent.

☆ C H A P T E R   T W O ☆

# The Third House
*House of Communication, Journeys, Brothers & Sisters*

The third house is often known as the house of communication. It contains one's capacity for gathering and sharing information. The areas that it includes are: knowledge the native possesses, short journeys, one's immediate environment, sisters and brothers and native's relationship with them. It also includes one's position and relations with friends. The house is also concerned with logic, memory and manual skills. It deals with the native's early education. Mercury being the natural ruler of the third house is associated with the sign Gemini. The skill of communication is not limited to talking but it relates to listening and perception, and other ways of communication too. If the third house is strong in a chart because benefic planets' have aspects on it, or its owner is placed in a good house, or its owner has aspects on it even if it is sitting in the 12$^{th}$ house, it will certainly benefit the native making him grow highly communicative, effortful, persuasive and help him to work constantly to achieve the determined goals.

We have analysed some natives' charts in which the owner of the third house is transiting in the 12$^{th}$ or the 6$^{th}$ house. The results are that the native has a small number of friends and less number of brothers or sisters. The native possesses ordinary communicative skills and he is not much effortful. But if any benefic planet is sitting in the third house, even though the owner of third house is in the 6th or 12th house, it makes the native extremely effortful, communicative, provides him good general education and gives many good friends. If the owner of the 3rd being Mars, sits even in the 12th house, (Virgo ascendant), it will have its aspects on the 3rd house which is its own house. In that case the native may not have any brothers or sisters, but will have a good number of friends, and will be highly effortful. Thus, the third house is very important for the progress of an individual.

If the owner of the third house is also the owner of the fourth house, eighth house or tenth house, the results will be excellent. But if the owner of the third house rules the sixth or twelfth house, the native will enjoy mixed results during his lifetime. Let us try to understand it with the help of a concrete example. A native born with Virgo as a rising sign has Mars, the ruler of the 3rd and the 8th placed in the 1st house (ascendant). It has made him highly effortful although he was once pushed to the brink of bankruptcy at the age of forty-four years on account of failure in his business. Besides, in the same chart Jupiter is also sitting in the third house that also makes the native highly effortful, communicative and gives him a good number of prestigious friends. Consequently, though he once reached the state of bankruptcy, he has recovered quite a lot within two years because both Jupiter and Mars are placed very favourably in his chart.*

*Thus, the reader must keep in mind that in view of good placement and lordship of the owner of the third house and favourable aspects on it will provide highly beneficial results*

---

* Please see the native's chart given as **Case Study Eight** on page 162 in our book, **Explore the Power of Astrology**.

*to the native. But besides the third house, if its owner also rules either the sixth or twelfth house, the native will enjoy only mixed results.*

We will be able to identify **certain precepts** in this respect for the benefit of the reader when we analyse a good number of birth-charts (*kundalis*) at the end of this chapter. Before we *broadly* discuss the effects of the transits of various planets in the third house, we wish to remind the reader to go through once again **what each house contains for us,** as without that knowledge the reader will not be able to analyse and identify the effects of the placements of various planets in different houses (See Appendix I). At the same time we would also like to remind the reader to keep in mind which signs the planets own (lordship) and in which signs they are exalted or debilitated. It is also imperative to keep in mind a planet's aspects on other houses (See Appendix II). Without all this knowledge a proper analysis or accurate prediction cannot be made.

# Transits of Planets

Let us now discuss the results of the transits of various planets in *the third house,* and examine their effects on a native keeping in mind their lordship and aspects on the particular houses. We have highlighted the text at the places where the planets' effects on an individual are specific and highly beneficial in a chart.

## *Sun Transiting the Third House*

The Sun's influence makes the native highly emphatic as regards his communication is concerned. It provides him leadership qualities as he is highly agile and effortful. The native has good connections and keeps friendship with the high ups in the government and political arena. He possesses a great desire to express himself in intellectual fields and gets good general education in his early life. The Sun placed in the third house makes the native a great communicator.

In fact, more will depend on the lordship of the Sun and its aspects in a chart when it is placed in the third house. In case it rules the 1st house (Leo-ascendant) and sits in the third, which is its debilitated sign (*Tula*), it will make the native effortful to some extent, but he may be harsh and curt in communication and keep the company of a few friends of ordinary status. At the same time the Sun's (exalted) aspects on the ninth house will make the native very lucky. At the age of 21 his luck will push him to great success in the field he is involved at that time. In case the Sun is the lord of the second house and sits in the third house, the native will earn money through artistic skills, teaching and professions related to broadcasting and communication. If the Sun sits in the third house and rules the fifth house, it will make the native highly communicative and provide him sons who will excel in speech and conversation. It is also possible that some of the native's children may choose law as their profession. The native may like to be an editor of a newspaper. If the Sun is the lord of the ninth or tenth house and sits in the third house, it will boost up the native's luck and provide him a job in the field of technology, engineering or communication, or he may look after the departments of broadcasting and communication as an engineer. If the Sun owns the eleventh house and is placed in the third house, it will make the native earn money through professions related to communication and public relations departments. It will also make him win people's support in political and social fields. He may be good in writing and speech. The native will be dashing and honest in conduct and output, and candid in speech. If the Sun owns the twelfth house and is placed in the third house, most of his efforts will be lost on account of his spendthrift conduct, irrational manner of dealing with the people and poor planning.

Thus, the reader must keep in mind two very important factors related to the Sun's placement in the third house. One is its lordship of a house in the chart, the other is its aspects on the ninth house. Predictions should be considered in view of the above two aspects.

## Moon Transiting the Third House

Under the influence of the Moon, the native cares a great deal for his family. He is highly interested in his educational expansion and travelling. The subject possesses a great curiosity to learn and has a strong imagination implicit with emotional thinking. Such a placement of the Moon will make the native restless, a good listener, possessing good memory. But more will depend on the Moon's ownership in a chart even though it sits in the third house.

Like the Sun which rules the sign Leo, the Moon also rules only one sign, Cancer. Let us briefly examine the results of the Moon's placement in the third house when it owns the other houses in a chart. If the Moon owns either the 6th, or the 8th or the 12th house, it may give bad results. But its lordship of any other house will only provide the native good results. For example, if it is placed in the 3rd and owns the 1st house, it will give benefits from sisters and women friends. It will also provide politeness in conduct, cultivating good communicative qualities and good imagination. If it owns the 2nd house, the native may do well with his family and may be less polite in speech. If it owns the 4th house, it will help in building a good house though a little late in life. It also gives him good imaginative qualities.

If it owns the 5th house, it will provide the native an excellent memory and a good educational career. It will also make the native excel in artistic qualities. His speech will be soft and he may have more number of daughters than sons. If it owns the 7th house, the native's partner will be highly educated and will help him in his endeavours. The native will be good in communication, both verbal and written. If it owns the 8th house, the native may have a great zeal in putting efforts to his job or business but due to highly imaginative tendencies, he might waste his efforts to some extent.

*If the Moon owns the 9th, 10th or 11th houses and sits in the 3rd house, it will bring good luck, favour from his lady boss and cultivate love for the navy as a career. It helps him earn good money and social status as well during the tenure of his service. Its ownership of the 9th house may give him opportunity to travel to foreign lands and bring good luck. If it owns the 10th house, it will provide him the opportunities of jobs related to sea or navy. When it owns the 11th house, it will make him popular with his community and bring riches at an early age. Moon's ownership of the 12th house will bring him waste in his efforts, and ignite bad relationship with friends.*

## Mars Transiting the Third House

Under the positive influence of Mars an individual will have a strong determination. He tries to get what he wants through persuasion and aggressive ways expressed through gestures and speech. Such a native is a quick thinker, especially when there is an emergency. An individual with a strong influence of Mars is strong physically and if he once takes decision, he likes to stay with it to a great extent.

Mars in the third house makes a native highly effortful, strong and frank in speech. He is highly communicative, daring, dashing in conduct, honest and persistent in pursuing his goals. As Mars rules Aries and Scorpio, it is necessary to examine the results of its ownership of various houses when it transits the third house. If it owns the ascendant (Aries) it makes the native skilful in technical knowledge. If it owns the ascendant (Scorpio) and sits in the third house, it gives the native very strong brothers who have high positions in government, military or police departments. He is a man of few words but very strong, aggressive, candid in communication, and enemies fear him. If it owns (Aries) the second house, the subject is good in communication, possesses artistic talents, good in speech, and brings good luck to the native the age of 21, 28 and 32 years.

When Mars sits in the third house (Aries), it makes the native strong willed, very effortful, consistent in following his missions in life, finds a good position in government, police or military department. From this position it also aspects the 6th, 9th and 10th houses. As a result, his enemies will always be subdued by him. He may be showy and artistic in his conduct and may take up acting as a profession. He may like medicine as his profession. If it owns the third house (Scorpio), it will provide him lots of manly qualities and will be full of strength and energy, lucky at the age of 32 years, can fare well in food and cloth-related business. When it owns the fourth house (Aries & Scorpio) and sits in the 3rd house, it helps him get riches, makes him good at speech, and gives good relationship with the mother; it provides the native good luck at the age of 21, and brings profit in medical and military equipments' sales. It also provides the native artistic qualities. The subject will be good in communication and speech too. When Mars owns the fifth house (Aries & Scorpio) and sits in the 3rd house, the native is good in learning and communicating scientific and technical knowledge, he is precise in explanations. This placement (Mars in Scorpio in the 5th) brings him stroke of luck first at 21 years, and later on makes him head of educational institutions; it also makes him highly communicative, attaining good general education. Often with such placements the native is inclined to join police department for his living.

When Mars owns the 6th house (Aries & Scorpio) and sits in the 3rd house, it helps the native to win over his opponents. He/she may choose surgery as a profession or career. The native can easily thrash his enemies. It makes him strong willed, attached and sincere to his job. If it owns the 7th house (Aries & Scorpio), luck may bring him success initially, fails seldom in efforts, may give him an educated wife who may support him in his progress. It may make him, at times, less effortful and lazy too. But he/she is lucky to get things with easy efforts. The native may like to choose to work in police department and may travel to distant lands. These results are more likely to happen when Scorpio sign rises in the 7th house as Mars bestows its exalted aspect on the 9th house from the 3rd house. If Mars owns the 8th house (Aries

& Scorpio) and sits in the 3$^{rd}$ house, it may make him highly effortful. The native may work in forest department, he may be highly agile, trustworthy, may earn money through illegal resources; it may also bring him great communicative qualities. This placement may make him highly eloquent as well as a good instructor or a teacher in medical, military or police academy.

*If Mars transits the 3$^{rd}$ house but owns the 9$^{th}$, 10$^{th}$ or 11$^{th}$ houses (Aries & Scorpio), it may develop the native's interest in dramatics and art-related professions. Such an individual is good in eloquence; he is resourceful and successful in joint ventures, winning against any kind of opposition. He gets occasional success in food-related business areas, and is liked by his own and other people; it is primarily a good placement to develop interest in art and dramatics, it may make the native polite in dealing with people and his co-workers as well.*

Mars transiting in the 3$^{rd}$ and having the lordship of the 12$^{th}$ house (Aries & Scorpio) may not give any brothers or sisters but may provide some good friends and make the native quite communicative and effortful. As it has an exalted aspect on the ninth house when Aries is rising in the 12$^{th}$ house, it makes the subject full of zeal, mostly inspired by envy and ambitions, and brings good luck at 21 and 32 years of age. It also provides a scientific outlook, a strong leaning towards achieving technological knowledge, quite successful in attaining education in early age, speaks less but speaks well, very practical and adventurous, and liked by his colleagues, co-workers and people.

## Mercury Transiting the Third House

Under the good influence of Mercury, an individual is lively and possesses an inquisitive mind. He is versatile and very capable in handling people and projects, especially literary and academic projects. He loves a lot of verbal give and take. Mercury placed in the 3$^{rd}$ house of an individual's chart provides him quick wit and good sense of humour. Such an individual is always eager to learn more. Its influence makes a subject restless. Professionally, the individual will like to be a writer, a reporter, an editor, a salesperson, a public relations officer, a counsellor and will always like to do more in his job.

When Mercury has the lordship of the 1$^{st}$ house (Gemini or Virgo & sits in the 3$^{rd}$) it is quite auspicious as it rules two houses, the 1$^{st}$ and 4$^{th}$ and the 10$^{th}$ and 1$^{st}$ houses. As such, it helps the native to attain good education at an early age, makes him good and precise in communication, emotionally attached to the mother and the native often builds a house at an early age; he inclines to be a teacher, has limited number of brothers and friends and is curt in his disposition at times. Mercury as the lord of the 2$^{nd}$ and the 5$^{th}$ houses (Gemini & Virgo) and placed in the 3$^{rd}$ house brings money, provides good family relationship, makes the native emotional in disposition, provides good memory and excellent attainment in education. Such a native is also blessed with more number of intelligent daughters who excel in their educational attainments.

*Mercury as the lord of 3$^{rd}$ and 6$^{th}$ houses (Gemini & Virgo) and placed in the 3$^{rd}$ house, is good as it gives good communicative abilities both in speech and writing, makes the native agile, skilful in editing and publishing, respectively. When Mercury owns the 7$^{th}$ and the 10$^{th}$ houses, and sits in the third house, it gives an intelligent, devoted and educated wife, who likes to walk with her husband. The native likes to be a teacher, editor, a writer and loves to work as a public relations officer.*

When Mercury owns the 8$^{th}$ and the 11$^{th}$ houses (Gemini & Virgo), it gives agility, plenty of physical zeal, courage and mobility; it also gives him a great social status, provides him riches through parents and grandparents. Mercury as the owner of the 12$^{th}$ and the 3$^{rd}$ houses (Gemini & Virgo) makes the native spend money on his brothers, sisters and friends. It makes him very popular among friends and relatives. His communicative abilities are excellent and he is very effortful.

## Jupiter Transiting the Third House

Jupiter is always considered a beneficial planet in the zodiac system. An individual under the positive influence of Jupiter will be a constructive thinker, an optimist, easily forgiving others, agile, less fault finding, always determined to pursue his aim in life, quite successful in marriage and partnership. Such a person often gets good luck through his mate but he always expects more from others. Such an individual is also a perfectionist in most of the matters in life and looks at things with a hopeful outlook.

*When Jupiter transits the third house and owns the 1st (Sagittarius) and the 4th houses (Pisces), it makes the individual very effortful, a pragmatic thinker having scientific temper, often provides an intelligent partner supporting the family financially, endowed with well placed brothers and good and faithful friends. Such an individual has a positive influence from his mother, but there is often delay in making a residence for the family.*

When Jupiter transits the 3rd house and owns the 10th (Sagittarius) and the 1st houses (Pisces), it may make the native highly imaginative, having a leaning towards arts and stage activities, mostly a daydreamer kind of person and often not able to complete his plans. When Jupiter is placed in the 3rd house and owns the 2nd and 5th houses (Sagittarius & Pisces), it provides good friends and supporting brothers; the individual has a scientific outlook, excellent memory, good educational attainments and a couple of sons who attain good education. When Jupiter is placed in the 3rd house and owns the 3rd and the 6th houses (Sagittarius & Pisces), it gives flourishing brothers and supporting and sincere friends. It provides good communicative abilities, helps earning good money through successfully completing projects. When Jupiter rules 4th and the 7th houses (Sagittarius & Pisces) and sits in the third house, it generally delays in making individual's own house, but relationship with the mother is good. It is often observed that with such a placement Jupiter makes the native impulsive in relation to his marriage. It also helps the native to earn a lot of money. When Jupiter is the lord of the 5$^{th}$ and the 8$^{th}$ houses (Sagittarius & Pisces) and is placed in the third house, it provides good education, a great zeal to lead life, straightforwardness in relationship and honesty in dealings with others and at the job. It also depends on the placement of the Sun (Leo ascendant) to assess how much the subject will fare in life, but normally such a native does very well and leads a respectable and socially approved life. He is also bestowed with gifted children who are well placed in life. When Jupiter owns the 6$^{th}$ and 9$^{th}$ houses (Sagittarius & Pisces) and is placed in the third house, it brings good luck to the native around 32 years of age, makes him highly communicative, quite affluent money-wise, but may have a partner slightly more in age than the native. It also gives the native frequent opportunities to travel abroad.

*When Jupiter owns 7$^{th}$ and 10$^{th}$ houses (Sagittarius & Pisces) and sits in the 3$^{rd}$ house, it provides a charming, i.e. loving and influential partner, makes the native highly influential and communicative. The native possesses good memory, a pleasing personality, is liked by his mates although he is often bossy. It is often observed that such a native inclines to be a teacher, a lawyer, a businessman dealing with cloth and garments, gems; and earns good money in life. Socially, he is very influential and at times he is also head of a department where he works.*

*Jupiter's placement in the 3$^{rd}$ house and having ownership of the 11$^{th}$ and the 2$^{nd}$ houses (Sagittarius & Pisces) will always be highly favourable financially. The native will be liked by his fellow workers and respected by the people in his community. He will also enjoy much respect in his family.*

## Venus Transiting the Third House

Venus is related to the artistic talents and signifies balance, sense of justice, and love for the people. It indicates a sophisticated disposition, feminine and affectionate temper, and inclines the native to love theatre, drama and arts. An individual having positive influence of Venus is often a compromiser, seeking harmony through communication. Such a native is charming and gentle, artistic, creative, possessing love for literature and poetry. He also seeks great pleasure in travelling.

When Venus transits the third house and rules the 1st and the 6th houses (Taurus & Libra), it makes the individual highly emotional, artistic, charming, seeking balance in life's activities, but at times sick with cold and careless in speech and expression.

*When Venus owns 2nd and 7th houses (Taurus & Libra) and sits in the 3rd, it makes the native highly communicative. Such a native has a beautiful wife who is highly cultivated, equipped with a logical bent of mind and helps him financially. The native is financially affluent and seeks his livelihood through artistic feats, likes to be a teacher of dance, art, or literature, or a painter.* The subject is highly sensuous and likes to indulge in sex games, mostly with educated ladies. In fact, he possesses an irresistible charm that attracts the opposite sex towards him. More will depend on Mars' placement in the birth-chart as Mars is the owner of the ascendant when Libra is rising in the 7th house. When Venus transits the third house and rules the 3rd and the 8th houses (Taurus & Libra), it certainly makes the native very sophisticated in speech and a great communicator.

*When Venus owns 4th and 9th houses (Taurus & Libra) and sits in the third house, the native's house construction plans are delayed, but his relationship with the mother is good. It provides luck in foreign lands. The native is very fond of long distance travelling and lives most of the time in foreign countries. He loves writing, teaching, editing, working in newspapers and loves music and musical concerts.* When Venus is the lord of the 10th and the 3rd houses (Taurus & Libra), it may develop native's interest towards jewellery, jobs relating to judiciary, revenue and broadcasting as the native possesses great communicative abilities. When Venus rules the 11th and the

4th houses (Taurus & Libra) and sits in the third house, the subject possesses a lot of land and his mother lives long. He is often in possession of great property, transport, personal vehicles, riches, and liked by the public. When Venus owns the 12th house either in Taurus or Libra and is placed in the 3rd, it is not a very healthy placement for it often brings dismay through weak finances, unnecessary expenditure and losses. Such an individual is less effective in speech and often incurs enmity through his curt disposition. However, he may have a devoted and affectionate wife as the sign Libra rises in the 12th house.

## Saturn Transiting the Third House

Saturn is a planet that is mostly misunderstood and often feared by those who don't really understand its proper role. It is the slowest moving planet in the zodiac system. Things happen slowly when its positive or negative influence is there in a chart. In fact, Saturn in the third house wants to help the native to learn things well so that he may use them at an appropriate time. It is a placement through which Saturn provides practical disposition. It helps the native to excel in mathematics or scientific knowledge. A subject with such a placement might work in a publishing, or communication-related industry. He can be a good accountant, a teacher, or a librarian. Such natives sometimes have problems with their neighbours and often have problems with their education at an early age. But the native possesses excellent power of concentration.

When Saturn owns the 1st and 2nd houses (Capricorn & Aquarius) and sits in the third house, it makes the native highly industrious and practical, who speaks less but he is quite judicious, and effective in speech. The native earns money through hard work and may like to work in a factory, industry or publishing company as a worker. When Saturn rules the 2nd and the 3rd houses (Capricorn & Aquarius), it gives riches and great communicative ability. The native is attached to his family and speaks judiciously. His early education is fairly well done. He is very effortful but much will depend on the placement of Jupiter in the chart, for Jupiter is the owner of the ascendant. If Jupiter is well placed, such a native could be very industrious and highly placed in life.

When Saturn sits in the third house and rules the 4th and 5th houses, it is beneficial for building a good residence, gives a couple of industrious and well placed sons, and a loving mother. If Venus is well placed in the native's chart he can be a great artist, a good teacher, interested in scientific knowledge in his early life and industrious too. When Saturn is the lord of the 5th and the 6th houses (Capricorn & Aquarius) and sits in the third house, it may benefit the native from vocations like publishing, printing and writing, and he may deal with material relating to medical or machinery. This placement may give him four sons who may be industrious and well placed in life in different vocations. It may help the native to get great success in life around the age of 32 years. When Saturn rules 7th and the 8th houses (Capricorn & Aquarius) and sits in the third house, it gives a caring partner, a long and healthy life and riches through relatives. It also provides an industrious partner who is bossy and talkative too.

*When Saturn owns 9th and 10th houses (Capricorn & Aquarius) and sits in the third house, the subject may possess an emotional disposition, like professions such as judiciary, law, teaching, printing and engineering. It may provide him good education in his early life. He may have leaning towards artistic vocations. The native in such placements will fare well in life as a law person and will feel comfortable only after the age of fifty. There is also a pretty good chance that he may lose his father at an early age, so he may have to struggle hard for everything in his early age.*

When Saturn transits the third house and owns the 10th and the 11th houses (Capricorn & Aquarius), it makes the native quite eloquent in speech, but his educational career is checked by such placement. He may not have children for a long time after marriage, but will have riches through business relating to transport, and selling material relating to machines. Saturn's ownership of the 12th and 1st houses may bring mixed results for it owns the 12th which is the house of expenditure and the 1st which is a very gainful house for any planet. But Saturn's aspects on the 9th house may bring him luck at the age of 32 and provide him opportunities to grow. Yet, at times, his expenditure may go beyond his income, making him doleful. As Saturn is in Mars' house (Aries) in the third, it may make him curt in speech and indulge in unnecessary enmity with brothers and friends.

### Rahu & Ketu Transiting the Third House

The placement of Rahu and Ketu (known as nodes or shadowy planets) in the third house, will bring results in view of their transits in a friend's or an enemy's sign. Except in Leo and Cancer which are not friendly signs to either of them, they are likely to bring good results to the native in almost all signs, making him industrious, quite conversant in speech, and benefiting him from brothers, sisters and friends. If either of the two transits a sign owned by Jupiter, they may give results in view of Jupiter's placement in the chart of the native. *The reader must understand that Rahu and Ketu are likely to provide good and beneficial results only if they transit in signs owned by Mercury and Venus, including Saturn, in an individual's chart.*

## Analysis of the Charts

It is now a proper opportunity to analyse actual charts (*kundalis*) of the subjects who have willingly handed them over to us for further explanations and predictions. *These charts will be examined in view of the strength and weakness of the individual's third house only.* We have similarly examined a good number of charts in our book, **Explore the Power of Astrology: Trikona One**, in relation to the 1st, 5th and 9th houses only.

# Case Study One

The following chart belongs to a Rajasthan-born person currently working in the UK in a senior position in a progressive bank.

**Native born on 10ᵗʰ January, 1977**

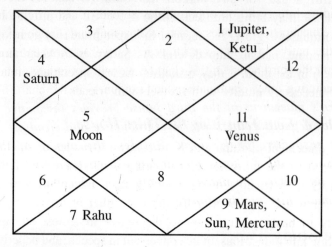

## *Broad Analysis*

Placement of the owner of the third, Moon, in the 4ᵗʰ house having aspects from Jupiter placed in the 12ᵗʰ, is excellent. It not only makes the native highly effortful, imaginative, caring for mother, but also provides him most of the benefits related to the 4ᵗʰ house, that is, building or purchasing a house mainly on account of the mother whom he adores, and also for the care of the father whom he also wants to help. He purchased a good flat in his native town almost at the end of 28 years of age when Jupiter was transiting in Libra and had aspects on both Venus (*lagnadhipati*) and Jupiter, owner of the 8ᵗʰ and the 11ᵗʰ. If you observe the native's chart, you will find Jupiter having aspects on the owners of the 4ᵗʰ, 5ᵗʰ & 7ᵗʰ from the beginning. It indicates that all these houses become strong and fruitful for the native. Besides, Venus, the owner of the ascendant, also aspects Moon that rules the 3ʳᵈ house. It also makes the 3ʳᵈ house very strong. Consequently, the native is highly effortful, imaginative, dutiful, and often has the company of damsels.

There is one more important factor worth noticing in the native's chart. It is the placement of Saturn in the 3rd house, which makes the native highly practical, steadfast and hard working. Saturn also has aspects on the 9th house. The aspect of the 9th lord on the 9th from the 3rd house benefits the native providing him good job opportunities abroad. It also offers him good education too. Besides, it also predicts long and short journeys that the native often takes each year. As we are concentrating only on the third house in this chapter, we will not indulge much in predicting other combinations and conjuncts in the chart, but *Saturn's placement in the third house provides the native a couple of good brothers who are productive and steadfast in their respective professions. Besides, the owner of the 9th rising in the 3rd house and having aspects on the 9th from there has helped the native to obtain good education abroad and made him highly effortful.*

## Case Study Two

The following is the chart of a great cricketer of India who remained at the top for almost two decades and relinquished captaincy voluntarily.

### Native born on 24th April, 1973

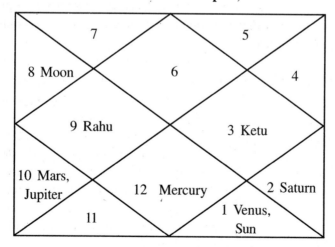

## Broad Analysis

The owner of the $3^{rd}$ sitting in an exalted position in the $5^{th}$ creates great opportunities in the field of sports for the native. Besides, the owner of the $11^{th}$ Moon sits in the $3^{rd}$ house giving him great financial benefits with his own dogged efforts. Jupiter, the owner of the $4^{th}$, conjuncts Mars, the owner of the $3^{rd}$. As such it has been providing the native mobile and immobile property-related benefits from the age of 16 years onwards. Again, a friendly aspect of Mars on the exalted Sun sitting in the $8^{th}$ house provides great agility to the native cultivating immense fighting capability in him. As a consequence, the native has excelled in his career bringing name to himself and to his country. The owner of the $3^{rd}$, Mars, sitting in an exalted position in the $5^{th}$, has given him great fortitude, capability to think and solve the problems. Consequently, playing intelligently when situations have demanded him to do so has always won him great respect from his team-mates as well as from the great cricketers abroad. Quite often he has been known as the Bradman of India. Aspects of the owner of the $3^{rd}$ on the $11^{th}$ house and owner of the $11^{th}$ on the $9^{th}$ have provided the native great luck, honour, fame, long foreign travels, and good education as well.

*Thus, the owner of the $3^{rd}$ if well placed in a chart can bring great name and wealth to the native, cultivating great respect for him through sports from people in his own country as well as abroad.*

## Case Study Three

The following chart belongs to a senior officer who retired from the position of Airport Manager a few years back. Now he is working as a manager in a progressive private travel agency.

# Native born on 3rd May, 1946

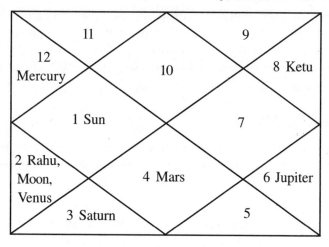

## Broad Analysis

There is an exchange between the owners of the 3rd and the 9th houses. Again, the owners of the ninth and the third houses also aspect each other. As a consequence both the houses have become very strong. The native has been highly effortful throughout his life and has also reflected a demeanour of friendship to most people he meets. He is a perfect combination of having good knowledge relating to his field, customer-oriented approach and problem-solving attitude. This made him very popular among his clients and with his co-workers within the airlines where he worked for more than thirty years before retirement.

There is one more good aspect on the third house of the native's chart. The ascendant, Saturn, sitting in the 6th house has its full aspect on the third house which makes the native highly agile, effortful, and friendly with the people. It also cultivates a habit of reading and acquiring new knowledge that provided him with confidence, initiative and dauntless and dashing conduct. Saturn's aspects on Mercury also makes the native very thoughtful, secretive and quite judicious. Placement of the exalted Sun in the 4th house of the native having aspects on the

10th house not only helped him to go up the ladder in his profession, it also provided him with great physical strength as well as ability to decide matters quickly. *It is a good example of a strong third house as the 3rd and the 9th have interchanged their positions with each other making both the 3rd and the 9th houses highly strong and fruitful by their mutual aspects.*

## Case Study Four

The following chart belongs to a promising young man who is working in a lucrative travel agency in Mumbai in India, and has been consistently very effortful in his job.

**Native born on 5th March, 1981**

```
        4 Rahu                    2
   5              3                    1

        6 Saturn,            12
        Jupiter
                                   11 Sun,
                                   Venus,
   7              9                Moon,
                                   Mars
        8          10 Ketu,
                   Mercury
```

*Broad Analysis*

In fact, when we observe the third house of the native we find that it has aspects from the Sun, Venus, Moon and Mars. Both the owners of the 3rd and the 5th are conjunct in the 9th house looking at the 3rd. The owner of the 11th, Mars, and the owner of the 2nd Moon, are also conjunct in the 9th and look at the 3rd. It makes the 3rd house very powerful. It provides the native good education in his early years, makes him very agile, effortful, friendly, hard working. Since both the owners of the $2^{nd}$ and the $11^{th}$ are conjunct in the $9^{th}$ and aspect the $3^{rd}$, it helps him to earn good money through honest efforts. He also loves to travel occasionally, which his job also requires from time to time. He is likely to have many good and trustworthy friends and a loving brother and sister as well. Not only that, the Sun, Mars and the Moon which are natural friends and are conjunct in a very auspicious house to bestow luck on the native, the Sun has also no adverse aspects from Saturn, its natural enemy. It is likely to provide a long life to his father and makes him love very intimately. Actually, the owners of the $9^{th}$ and the $10^{th}$, Saturn and Jupiter, are conjunct in the $4^{th}$ house and have aspects on the $10^{th}$. It makes quite a strong **Rajyoga** that provides him the benefit of a good residence, mobile property and progress in his career. Except that the owner of the ascendant is sitting in the $8^{th}$ house with Ketu and Saturn has aspects on the ascendant, *most of the yogas and aspects on the $3^{rd}$ house are quite promising, bringing him good luck, scientific temperament, making him highly effortful, energetic and bringing riches*. From the age of 27 years until 34 years, both progress and position are bound to come to him.

## Case Study Five

The chart on the next page belongs to a senior scientific officer working in a State's Mines Department. He is well known for his kind and friendly disposition as well as for hard and good work in his department.

## Native born on 30th July, 1956

```
┌─────────────────────────────────────────┐
│         4 Sun,                           │
│         Mercury          2 Ketu          │
│   5                                      │
│   Jupiter      3  Venus        1  Moon   │
│                                          │
│          6              12               │
│                                          │
│   7             9              11 Mars   │
│        8  Saturn,                        │
│           Rahu          10               │
└─────────────────────────────────────────┘
```

## Broad Analysis

The owner of the 3rd Sun is conjunct with the owner of the 1st house, Mercury, in the second house that makes the native ethical, conversant and pleasant in speech and provides him a good family background. Jupiter's placement in the 3rd being the owner of the 10th has added to the strength of the 3rd as well as given him an opportunity to work in a good position in a very lucrative State government department. Besides, the owner of the 11th, Mars, has also its auspicious aspect on the 3rd, making the native very effortful, providing good early education. Jupiter sitting in the 3rd aspects two very important houses in the native's chart—the 7th and the 11th, which provides him benefits from a very caring and educated wife and by giving him a good heart (aspects on Moon) and advantage to earn money by honest means. In fact, the owner of the ascendant, Mercury, transiting the 2nd and the Moon being the owner of the 2nd rising in the 11th, has made a kind of *Laxmi Yoga* which gives the native benefit of possessing a lot of money.

As the owner of the 11th Saturn has aspects on Jupiter, the owner of the 10th house, it indicates good financial benefits from his job and job-related matters. Since Saturn, the owner of the 9th, aspects Jupiter, it gives him a good position in his department, except that some of his colleagues would be his critics too and cultivate ill feelings against him. Jupiter being the owner of the 7th and 10th and transiting the 3rd house has several beneficial influences on the native. Not only his mate is highly intelligent and cooperative, she has always assisted him in his life and helped the family to grow positively. *Besides, Jupiter's beneficial aspects on its natural friends Mars and Moon has given him great strength of character and a kind as well as helping heart. This makes the third house strong in its own manner as not only its owner is well placed, the house also has good aspects from the yogakarak planets.*

## Case Study Six

The following chart belongs to a promising future engineer who is in the final stages of passing out around May 2007.

### Native born on 9th March, 1986

*Broad Analysis*

*The owner of the 3rd, Saturn, conjunct with the ascendant Mars at the ascendant provides the native with extraordinary pragmatic qualities that would bring great success in life. It makes him very hard working, result oriented, dashing, and quite trustworthy, but secretive as well.* He will be endowed with very affectionate sister and brother and a loving and educated mother. The owner of the 3$^{rd}$, Saturn also aspects the 3$^{rd}$ from the *lagna,* which confirms all the qualities and characteristics as stated above.

Saturn sitting at the ascendant has aspects on the 7$^{th}$ as well as on the 10$^{th}$ houses besides its aspects on the 3$^{rd}$. It helps the native to get a good and an artistic kind of a mate who would be caring and loving. As far as Saturn's aspects on the 10$^{th}$ house are concerned, it gives him opportunity to work in private companies and also suggests changing a couple of jobs in his professional career. Well, the owner of the 7$^{th}$ is already exalted in the fifth house, which indicates some kind of love marriage or having known the mate beforehand. There is a great alliance of the three friendly planets in the chart, i.e., the Sun, the Moon and Jupiter, which are conjunct at the 4$^{th}$ house. This sort of conjunct is highly beneficial to the native as the owner of the 10$^{th}$ is conjunct with the owners of the 5$^{th}$ and the 9$^{th}$. This conjunct is a great *yogakarak* which will provide him benefits and offers of good jobs, leading to acquiring a lot of land and property. It is going to boost up the native's luck at an early age and may offer great opportunities starting from 21 years until 28 years and later on too.

## Case Study Seven

The following chart belongs to a famous law books publisher at Gujarat in India. He has good connections with the State's leading politicians and intellectuals for a pretty long time.

## Native born on 25th October, 1951

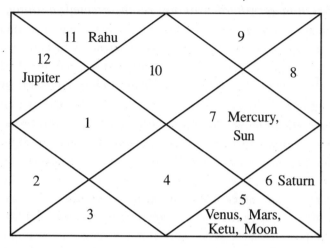

## Broad Analysis

When we analyse the 3rd house in the above chart, it indicates native's friendly nature that led him to possess good friends throughout his life, including a loving brother and sister. It also suggests expenditure incurred on friends and relatives. *Actually, the ascendant, Saturn, and the owner of the 3rd Jupiter are sitting in opposition. It is a very strong kind of drishti yoga. It means both the ascendant and the owner of the 3rd house have strong aspects on each other. It suggests that the native will be highly effortful, have political links, will be very practical, farsighted, and result oriented in his output. A highly beneficial Saturn, rising in a friendly sign in the 9th house has aspects on the 3rd house and its owner, Jupiter.* It has boosted up the native's luck since the age of 33 years and has brought him most of the success he achieved in life.

When we observe the chart carefully, we find that Mars, owner of the 11th and the 4th sitting in the 8th, also aspects Jupiter. It provides a very strong will to the native. Once if he determines to take up a project he would surely complete it. That kind of attitude has mostly benefited the native in life. In fact, the

Sun-Mercury conjunct in the 10th house indulge him in printing and paper work. Besides, the Sun has its exalted aspects on the 4th house which suggests possession of a great mansion, land as well as mobile property. Jupiter, being a naturally benefic planet, has its positive aspects on the ascendant. It has provided a very pious and respectful demeanour, cultivating compassion and a helping attitude in him. As the ascendant has beneficial aspects on it, it always helps the native to cultivate a positive kind of thinking, bringing him solace and religiosity within. Except that the Moon, the owner of the 7th, is conjunct and is afflicted by Ketu, which provides him heart-related illness around 56 to 58 years of age, other *yogas* are highly beneficial. When Saturn transits in Virgo by the end of 2009, he will recover health-wise. Jupiter will also have good aspects on the ascendant at that time which suggests good recovery from illness, and good health.

## Case Study Eight

The following chart belongs to a Section Officer in a Central Government office. His position in the office demands him to deal with people. He fulfils that demand very skilfully by his polite demeanour. As such he is quite popular and influential.

### Native born on 24th October, 1971

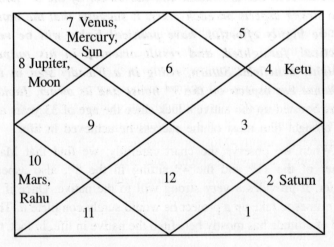

## Broad Analysis

*The placement of a beneficial Jupiter in the $3^{rd}$ house, being the owner of the $4^{th}$ and the $7^{th}$, has added to the strength of the $3^{rd}$ house by making the native extremely hard working and productive. The Moon rules the $11^{th}$ and is conjunct with Jupiter in the $3^{rd}$ house in the native's chart. It yields him financial benefits through his planning and hard work. Saturn, the owner of the 5th, sitting in the 9th house, also aspects the $3^{rd}$ house providing him quite a pragmatic ability to sort out his projects well and to complete them on time and fruitfully too. Mars, the owner of the $3^{rd}$ is sitting in the $5^{th}$ in an exalted sign. It makes the native further agile, highly effortful and goal-oriented.*

The native, being a Section Officer in a Central Government Department, has to be very commanding and influential in his office. He possesses all such qualities not only because of his position in the office but because of the placement of the planets in his chart. Overtly he might look an easy-going person (because Mercury and Venus conjunct in the $2^{nd}$) but within he is disciplined, and is able to control the office as the situation warrants. Saturn not only aspects the $3^{rd}$ house but also the $11^{th}$ and the $6^{th}$ houses. It provides him the insight to get benefits from the projects in his control. Besides, Jupiter also has its aspects on the $11^{th}$ house, providing him financial benefits in his job and support from the public he deals with. Good aspects from Jupiter on the $7^{th}$ house, while sitting in the $3^{rd}$, provides him benefits from a very caring wife, who is highly family-oriented, loving, truthful to him and helpful in the progress of the family. The owner of the $3^{rd}$ Mars sitting in an exalted position in the $5^{th}$ provides him a very lucky and promising son who will be *kuldeepak* for his family. Most probably he will either be a doctor or an engineer and will be highly successful in his career. When analysis of the native's chart is being made (early 2007) Jupiter is transiting in the sign Scorpio, which is also his nativity. It should prove an excellent year for the native as far as good finances and benefits from the projects are concerned.

# Case Study Nine

The following chart belongs to a secondary school student studying in a leading institute. He has already distinguished himself in Tennis at an early age at the school level.

**Native born on 28ᵗʰ December, 1990**

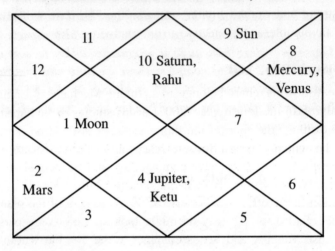

## Broad Analysis

*The owner of the 3ʳᵈ Jupiter exalts in the 7ᵗʰ house and aspects the 3ʳᵈ, 11ᵗʰ and the 1ˢᵗ houses. As such it makes the native very determined and hard working. Saturn is the owner of the ascendant and aspects the 3ʳᵈ house. It provides the native farsightedness, practical ability and job oriented demeanour.*

Mars and the Sun are friendly in the chart. Mars is rising in the 5ᵗʰ and aspects the Sun in the 12ᵗʰ house which rises in its friend's sign. It also provides the native the physical strength required by a sportsman. In fact, Mars has helped the native to excel in sports at an early age, but good aspects of Jupiter on the 3ʳᵈ also make him agile, hard working as well as highly productive. Right now (2007) Jupiter is transiting the native's 11ᵗʰ house. It provides him the required inspiration and agility as it aspects Mars (provider of the sportsman's qualities) from the 11ᵗʰ house.

It is hoped that the current year will prove a landmark in his life as far as sports and studies are concerned. It is simply on account of the placement of Rahu and Ketu at the ascendant and in the 7th house respectively that some of the good results narrated here above may not be fully realised by the native as both these shadowy planets do yield negative results from time to time. But a strong and exalted Jupiter sitting in the 7th house will always be favourable and protective to the native.

## Case Study Ten

The following chart belongs to a future Mechanical Engineer studying in the fourth year (2007) of his studies in Maharashtra. We examine the chart of the future engineer just to find out how far he will put good efforts to reach the desired goals in life.

### Native born on 18th October, 1984

*Broad Analysis*

*Saturn, the owner of the 3rd is transiting in the 12th house at the time of the native's birth. As such, though Saturn is in an exalted sign, it brings some kind of lethargic attitude towards work and makes the native less effortful although he may possess strong desires to fulfil great things in life.*

It is on account of the placement of the ascendant Mars in the 2nd house along with Jupiter, the owner of the 5th, that the native will work hard to move up only at the time of dire need. It is also not quite favourable that the owner of the 10th, Sun, is sitting with Saturn in the 12th house. It is not promising as far as job opportunities are concerned and also not healthy as far as his relationship with his father is concerned. He will be changing several jobs with no obvious reasons. Besides, Mercury, the owner of the 11th, is also sitting in the 12th house with Saturn. It adversely affects the native's financial benefits. Venus, as the owner of the 7th and 12th houses, rises at the ascendant at the time of the native's birth. It makes the native quite a spendthrift, mainly on account of keeping friendship with opposite sex and also due to his mate after he is married. It (Venus) also promises good luck through the mate.

*The Moon, as the owner of the 9th, is sitting in the 9th. It provides the native luck and imaginative qualities as it aspects the 3rd from the 9th house. It also gives him some agility to move and to fulfil the desired goals to some extent.*

Saturn, having aspects on the Moon, affects the native's emotional life and bridles his luck to some extent. Besides, Saturn also aspects Mars from the 12th house, which is quite favourable to the native as it has helped him to choose engineering as a profession. The conjunct of Mars and Jupiter as the owners of the 1st and the 5th is highly beneficial to the native as it helps him attain good and desired educational goals in life although Saturn's aspects on both of these benefic planets diminishes the good effects of Mars and Jupiter to a certain extent. The native needs to bridle his emotional flights at the time of his marriage for the ties made in a hurry might not bring him as good results as expected.

## Case Study Eleven

The following chart belongs to an industrialist based in Indore who has enjoyed married life for more than fifty years when (2007) his chart is being analysed. He possesses riches and great social status earned by dedication to his work that he discharged with honesty and sincerity.

**Native born on 12th August, 1932**

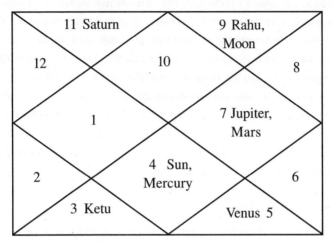

## Broad Analysis

It is one of the very good examples of an astrological chart that reflects strong 3rd, 11th and 1st houses. Consequently, on account of these important houses being strong in the chart, the native rose to a very high position in life and earned lots of money, possessed a great social status and commanded great reputation among his relatives and people at the workplace. The owner of the 3rd house, Jupiter, though transiting in its enemy sign, has gained strength as it is conjunct with its natural friend Mars, which has an exalted aspect on the ascendant. Mars as the owner of the 11th and the 4th is conjunct with Jupiter, the owner of the 3rd. Mars also aspects the ascendant with its exalted aspect. It is conjunct in the 10th house with Jupiter, the owner of the 3rd. It provided the native great agility and strength in discharging his duties and responsibilities. Yet there is another important factor worth noticing in the chart. A strong Saturn, owner of the ascendant, is transiting the 2nd house in the chart and has its aspects on the 11th house which is also the house of riches. Jupiter also has aspects on Saturn. All such aspects and conjuncts form *Laxmi Yoga* that bestows upon the native riches, honour and social status.

*Therefore, before assessing the strength of a house, the reader must keep in view various sorts of aspects and conjuncts. If a particular house and its strength is being assessed, one must keep these points in mind as to what sort of aspects that house has and how strong is the ascendant in the chart. Then the aspects and the conjuncts should also be of friendly nature. For example, in the above chart, though Jupiter is not rising in its friendly sign, it is conjunct with Mars which is one of its permanent friends. Besides, Mars has its exalted aspect on the ascendant too. Therefore, the native has always been extremely effortful and productive in his life.*

## Case Study Twelve

The following chart belongs to a senior secondary school student who is about to appear in the final examination at the time (March, 2007) her chart is being analysed. She intends to become a psychiatrist and hopes to join medical services. Let us examine her chart and see how much efforts she can put to attain her goal in life.

### Native born on 29th March, 1989

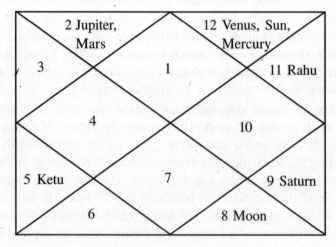

## Broad Analysis

When we examine the 3rd house of the native, we find that it is rising in the 12th conjunct with an exalted Venus along with the Sun. Not only that, the owner of the 3rd, Mercury, is in its debilitation sign; it is rising in the 12th house which is the house of waste, travels and of expenditure. That indicates that her efforts might be wasted even though the owner of the 3rd is conjunct with its permanent friend, Venus. Traditional astrology reckons that the 5th house is related to education and projects. As the Sun is also conjunct with Mercury in the 12th, it also suggests less success in her education. But modern and Western astrologers suggest that attainment of higher and good education depends upon the placement and ownership of the 9th house. In the native's chart, the owner of the 9th Jupiter is placed in the 2nd along with Mars, which is the owner of the ascendant. It is a kind of silver lining in her chart. Although Jupiter also owns the 12th house and is sitting in the 2nd in a sign that is not friendly, it is conjunct with Mars, which is the owner of the ascendant. Mars being the owner of the 1st and the 8th bestows on the native determination and zeal, which may be helpful in attaining her goal in life.

*There is one more factor that needs the reader's attention. It is the placement of Saturn in the 9th house having its aspects on the 11th, 3rd and the 6th houses. Since Saturn is a natural friend of Mercury, it is going to restore the lost strength of the 3rd house by its aspects. Besides, its aspects on the 11th also indicate riches in life. An exalted Venus, though in the 12th but being the owner of the 7th and conjunct with Mercury, also suggests better results, except it indicates some kind of difficulties in her married life. Above all, it is the Sun-Mercury conjunct which could be further helpful in attaining good education.*

Thus, it seems that initially she might not be successful, but if she goes on trying after one or two failures she can be successful finally. The best time to attain her goals could be when Jupiter transits the sign Scorpio (which is in 2007) or Sagittarius (Nov. 2008) and has its aspects on Mercury, the 1st house and on the 5th house as well.

## Brief Summary of Results

*Thus, the reader must keep in mind two very important factors relating to planets' placements in the third house. One is its lordship in the chart and the other is good and bad aspects on that house. Predictions should be considered in view of the above two aspects. For example, Mercury as the lord of 3rd and 6th houses (Gemini & Virgo) and placed in the 3rd house is good as it gives good communicative abilities both in speech and writing, makes the native agile, skilful in editing and publishing, respectively.*

*When Jupiter, as the owner of the 3rd house, exalts in the 7th house and aspects the 3rd, 11th and the 1st houses, it bestows beneficial results. It makes the native very determined and hard working. The placement of a beneficial Jupiter in the 3rd house, being the owner of the 4th and the 7th, adds to the strength of the 3rd house by making the native extremely hard working and productive.*

*The Moon, as owner of the 11th, if conjuncts with Jupiter in the 3rd house, it brings very fruitful results. It yields financial benefits through good planning and hard work. If Mars owns the 3rd house and sits in the 5th in an exalted sign, it makes the native further agile, highly effortful and goal-oriented, and excelling in sports and such activities.*

*Saturn, as the owner of the ascendant, if aspects the 3rd house, also makes the native very hard working and determined. It provides the native farsightedness, practical ability and job-oriented demeanour. Saturn as the lord of the 5th house, when rises in the 9th house, has its aspects on the 3rd house. It provides the native quite a pragmatic ability to sort out his projects well and to complete them on time and fruitfully too. When Saturn as the owner of the 3rd is conjunct with the ascendant Mars at the ascendant, it provides the native with extraordinary pragmatic qualities that would bring greater success in life. It makes him very hard working, result-oriented, dashing, and quite trustworthy, but secretive as well.*

*A good example of a strong third house could be when the owners of the 3rd and the 9th have interchanged their positions. It provides a lot of strength to each other's houses, making them both (the 3rd and the 9th houses) highly strong and fruitful on account of their mutual aspects.*

## The Seventh House
### House of Romance, Marriage & Legal Affairs

**W**estern astrological traditions unfold that the seventh house relates to your partner and marriage. Its natural sign is Libra, which is associated with Venus. It indicates what kind of mate and marriage you will have. It also indicates other partnerships— business partnerships, including your legal affairs and agreements as well. A successful analysis of this house may also indicate your shared goals and commitments towards your mate, friends and business partners. In fact, it is a house of your primary relationship that includes everything, from your soul mate to your close friends, including how you cooperate and share your feelings while working with others.

Indian traditions reckon that the seventh house is mainly related to your spouse, your mate and your partnership in business or any other project that is instrumental for your growth and progress. Besides, the 7th house is taken into consideration when assessing one's *markesh* or time and yoga for one's death. In this section we are not dealing with *markesh* because to calculate the time of death, besides the 7th house one's 2nd house and the *maha-dasha* periods are also taken into account. Let us now examine the transits of various planets through the seventh house and identify their good and bad effects on a native in relation to the 7th house.

## Transits of Planets

When different planets transit through the seventh house in a chart, they affect the native's activities relating to that house. Especially, when Saturn, Jupiter, Rahu & Ketu transit through it, they certainly influence the native's activities relating to the seventh house. It is because planets like Jupiter and Saturn, including the nodes Rahu & Ketu, stay in a sign for a considerably long time. For example, Jupiter transits in one sign for almost one year, whereas Saturn stays in a sign for two and a half years. Rahu & Ketu transit backwards in a sign for almost one and a half years. All other planets stay almost for one and a half months in a sign, except the Sun and the Moon that stay in a sign for one month, and two and a half days respectively. Besides, most planets, except the Sun and the Moon, retrograde in a sign sometimes in a year, giving the retrograding planet some kind of special energy or strength. When predictions are made relating to a particular planet transiting in a house, it needs to be kept in mind whether that planet is retrograding. If it would be the case, the planet's retrograding state should be kept in view before making any predictions. (See Appendix IV about retrograding planets.)

### Sun Transiting the Seventh House

When the Sun transits the seventh house it generally influences matrimonial matters, including any kind of business deals. The Sun's good and bad effects on an individual (when transiting the seventh house) can be seen in the light of the aspects from the beneficial and malefic planets on the seventh house.

When the Sun transits the seventh house and owns the 1st house, it may delay marriage matters but it is a good placement for the individual as it gives him strength of conviction and strong will except that the individual may be stubborn in nature. If the Sun owns the 2nd house, it may affect the native's household affairs and he may be curt and unpleasant in speech. His relationship with the members of family may not be as good as it should be. If the Sun owns the 3rd house and transits the seventh, it is a very positive placement as it helps the native to have good business partners, good company of friends, and a caring spouse. If the Sun owns the 4th house and transits the seventh, it helps to build a house at 31 years of age. It will come true if Jupiter has its aspects on the 4th or the 7th house. If the Sun owns the 5th house and sits in the seventh, it may give one son to the native and may disturb relationship with the spouse. If the Sun owns the 6th house, it may give an educated partner who may be a bigmouth and indulge in discussions with the native time to time. He has to be careful in making business partnerships if he has any. If the Sun owns the 7th house, it is not a good placement as the ascendant occupies the sign Aquarius. It may cause constant problems with the partners and the spouse. If it owns the 8th house and sits in the seventh, it may divert the native's attention towards sports activities and may delay the marriage.

*If it sits in the seventh and owns the 9th house, it is a great placement as it owns the house of luck. It helps the native through his spouse, who is often caring and loving, supports the native financially as well as in social and family matters. If the Sun owns the 10th house and sits in the seventh, it may cultivate artistic qualities and gives a very caring and loving partner. When the Sun owns the 11th house it helps financially through the spouse and makes the native popular and socially respected.*

When the Sun owns the 12th house and sits in the seventh house it may delay the native's marriage and may also give him a partner who is a spendthrift and less adjusting to the native.

## Moon Transiting the Seventh House

When the Moon owns the seventh house it gives an emotional relationship with the partner and makes the native quite attached to the spouse. As the Moon also aspects the ascendant from the seventh, it indulges the native in flights of imagination and makes him less pragmatic.

When the Moon owns the 1st house and sits in the seventh house it provides a loving wife and his relationship with his business partners is more on an emotional level than pragmatic. When the Moon owns the 2nd house, it provides a soothing tongue and positive relationship with the members of his family. When it owns the 3rd house it provides a homogeneous relationship with the partner but makes the native imaginative and artistic in vision. He is also decently communicative. When the Moon owns the 4th house it helps the native to build good relationship with the mother and provides him an opportunity to build a house at 28 years of age. When it owns the 5th house, it tends to provide the native more number of daughters and gives him a good memory and imaginative talents.

When the Moon owns the 6th house, it incites enmity with his partners and relatives, makes him highly sensuous and arrogant. When the Moon occupies the 7th house, it provides a very emotional partnership but it may also give occasional problems with the partner as he may be too dogmatic in his approach and outlook. When the Moon owns the 8th house and sits in the seventh, it gives an educated partner who may outwit the native in speech and action.

*If the Moon owns the 9th house and sits the 7th house, it becomes very auspicious as it is in its exalted sign, provided Jupiter is also well placed in the chart. In that case it will help in boosting up the native's luck at the age of 21 years, will give an artistic kind of spouse, who may be very loving and attached to him emotionally. The native will also have good relationship with his business partners. But he may be conceited in nature as the Moon has debilitated aspects on* *the ascendant. The 10<sup>th</sup> and 11<sup>th</sup> house ownership of the Moon are good job-wise and financially respectively. It may give him an opportunity to work in the navy, or water-related professions and the native might be helped financially by his working spouse.*

The Moon as the owner of the 12<sup>th</sup> house (sitting in the 7<sup>th</sup>) may delay the native's marriage and disturb relationship with business partners. It is not quite a very welcoming placement of the Moon.

## Mars Transiting the Seventh House

Mars remains highly independent even in relationship and it is usually the one who begins those relationships impulsively, emotionally and aggressively. When there are adverse aspects on Mars in the seventh house, it indicates more than one marriage. It has been observed that Mars in the seventh house makes a person quarrelsome, mostly because the individual likes to move in his own way. It is also observed that when Mars is placed in the seventh house, it may give an aggressive or emotional partner. But when Mars has good aspects, it may make the native highly cooperative and he is good with major relationships and the people he works with.

When Mars transits through the seventh house and has the lordship of the 1<sup>st</sup> and the 8<sup>th</sup> houses (Aries & Scorpio), it may provide a strong will and great flow of energy in the native, but his relationship with his partner may not be very congenial unless there are benefic aspects on the seventh house. It may also make the subject dogged in nature, unbending on matters he thinks he is right. When Mars is the lord of the 2<sup>nd</sup> and the 9<sup>th</sup> houses (Aries & Scorpio) one gets one's luck boosted through one's mate who is highly cooperative. It also provides a couple of worthy sons who may not have very congenial relationship with the subject but are quite successful in life.

*When Mars owns the 3<sup>rd</sup> and the 10<sup>th</sup> houses (Aries & Scorpio) and sits in the seventh, it is a great placement as* *regards individual's luck, early education and effortful career is concerned but his partner may be stiff, unbending and less cooperative: as such, he may marry again. He is likely to get great success in life between 28 to 33 years. When Mars sits in the seventh and owns the 4th and 11th houses (Aries & Scorpio), it is also quite a lucrative placement which makes the individual highly well placed in science, technology or medical fields, provides him a loving and caring mother and lots of property, job-wise great success in the areas controlled or influenced by Mars, but his married life may not be very happy unless the seventh house has aspects from Jupiter.*

When Mars owns the 5th and the 12th houses (Aries & Scorpio) it may give mixed results as it makes the spouse a spendthrift, highly communicative, persuasive but less cooperative, clever and socially well placed. The native may have a couple of sons on whom he has to spend a lot of money and efforts to settle them in life. When Mars owns the 6th and the 1st houses (Aries & Scorpio) and sits in the seventh house, it also gives mixed results as it provides quite a dashing personality and may give him an artistic kind of mate, but his relationship with the business partners may not be very good and may be leading to occasional skirmishes and unhappiness.

## Mercury Transiting the Seventh House

Mercury seeks intellectual compatibility both in marriage and partnerships. It gives great communicative abilities. There is a lot of verbal give and take, and the native is highly successful, particularly in professions like law, literature, writing, teaching, and communications. Besides, he can also be successful as a salesperson, public relations officer, and as an arbitrator. When Mercury has good aspects on it, it can help in cultivating good relationship with people and the partner but when it has bad aspects, it may lead to misunderstandings and unfulfilled agreements. Such a native loves to marry a highly intellectual partner who is well educated.

*When Mercury owns the 1^st and the 4^th houses (Gemini & Virgo) and sits in the seventh, it provides an intelligent and intellectual personality, a loving mother, lots of property from the parents, a cooperative and loving partner and good relationship with the business partners, and helps building a house at the age of 28 or 31 years.*

When Mercury rules the $2^{nd}$ and the $5^{th}$ houses (Gemini & Virgo) and sits in the seventh house, it helps to earn through teaching, speech-related jobs like law or a public relations officer. He may have a mate who is aggressive and emotionally unbalanced. When Mercury owns $3^{rd}$ and the $6^{th}$ houses and sits in the $7^{th}$ house, it is a good placement to have an artistic mate and helps to possess highly communicative abilities. The native will like to be a publisher and will be happy to work as a teacher, a writer or may work in printing departments. He may have one son who will be well placed in life.

*When Mercury owns the 7^th and the 10^th houses (Gemini & Virgo) and sits in the 7^th house, it helps to get a highly educated and communicative partner, it provides good relationships with the business partners and inclination to have jobs relating to food or cloth, teaching, publishing and editing fields.*

When Mercury owns $8^{th}$ and $11^{th}$ houses (Gemini & Virgo), it gives a partner who has artistic talents, is highly social, caring and loving. The native has good contacts and is respected socially. Besides, he earns good money through art and acting-related vocations, including teaching and medical professions. When Mercury owns $9^{th}$ and $12^{th}$ houses (Gemini & Virgo) and is placed in the seventh house, it provides luck through the partner, who is a spendthrift and possesses a bigmouth.

*When Mercury owns the 10^th and the 1^st houses (Gemini & Virgo), it is quite a wholesome placement though Mercury is in its debilitated sign in the seventh house. It provides a pleasing personality having liking for teaching, love for communication-related jobs, interest in cloth, food, printing and publishing-related areas, and great success in them. He may also have a partner who is more matured but also endowed with artistic abilities, and is very pleasing and loving. As Mercury has its exalted aspect on the ascendant from the seventh house, it may provide great liking for him from a great number of people.*

## Jupiter Transiting the Seventh House

When Jupiter transits the seventh house it is very helpful in matrimonial relationships and business partnerships. It also indicates more than one marriage. With such a placement the partner is optimistic and often brings good fortune and financial benefits. The native's dealings with the members of his family and others is always good.

*When Jupiter owns the 1ˢᵗ and 4ᵗʰ houses (Sagittarius & Pisces) and is placed in the 7ᵗʰ house, it provides the native a charming personality and people respect him, as he is honest and straightforward. His relationship with his mother is good and he is the owner of a good house mostly provided by his parents. The spouse is highly educated, supporting and loving. His communicative capabilities, both in speech and writing, are often praiseworthy.*

When Jupiter owns the 2ⁿᵈ and the 5ᵗʰ houses (Sagittarius & Pisces) and sits in the seventh, it makes the native possess a straightforward manner of speech, honest in dealings with relatives, and a couple of good sons who are well placed in life. When Jupiter owns the 3ʳᵈ and the 6ᵗʰ houses (Sagittarius & Pisces), it makes the native highly communicative, effortful but he does not have quite smooth relationship with his business partners.

*When Jupiter owns the 7ᵗʰ and the 10ᵗʰ houses (Sagittarius & Pisces) and is in the 7ᵗʰ, it is considered as a great placement. It gives a good and devoted wife and a prestigious job. It also makes the native very agile and quick in his work and dealings. It is one of the best placements of Jupiter.*

*When Jupiter owns the 8th and the 11th houses (Sagittarius & Pisces) and is placed in the 7th, it gives great physical strength and the native is helped financially by his spouse. He is also respected by relatives and by people in his community.*

As far as spouse's help and cooperation is concerned, much will also depend on the beneficial placement of Mars in the chart. When Jupiter owns the 9th and the 12th houses (Sagittarius & Pisces) and is placed in the seventh house, it provides good luck occasionally but poor relationship with the spouse, who is often a spendthrift and is less cooperative with him. Socially he is liked less and his wife constantly stands in opposition to him.

## Venus Transiting the Seventh House

When Venus transits the seventh house, it provides a cooperative and loving partner, who has artistic tastes and inclination. His relationship with his business partners is often wholesome and he is financially well off. In both the cases when Taurus or Libra is rising at the seventh house, the ascendant is owned by Mars. As such the native has inclination towards drama and acting, and has a practical outlook towards life.

When Venus owns the 1st and the 6th houses (Taurus & Libra) and rises in the seventh house, it gives a charming and young spouse who is aggressive in conduct and often dominating. When Venus owns the 2nd and the 7th houses (Taurus & Libra), it helps the native financially. The spouse brings him luck and money. She is artistic and often attached with some kind of cultural activities bringing honour to the family. When Venus owns the 3rd and the 8th houses (Taurus & Libra), it makes the native very communicative and provides him energy and zeal to work for the good of the people.

*When Venus owns the 4th and the 9th houses (Taurus & Libra), and sits in the 7th, it is quite a beneficial placement financially and property-wise. It helps bringing good luck to the native at the age of 32 years, though the native's relationship with his spouse is not quite wholesome as she is rigid, occasionally curt but ethical in her outlook and conduct.*

When Venus owns the 5th and the 10th houses (Taurus & Libra) and sits in the 7th, it gives intelligent daughters, but his relationship with his mate is often at fence. She may choose to be a teacher, a surgeon or an engineer and may be less cooperative with the native. If Venus owns the 6th and the 11th houses (Taurus & Libra), and sits in the 7th, it may help in finances, boost social prestige, cultivate good relationship with the people in politics and may provide quite an intelligent partner who is good in communication and caring. When Venus owns the 12th and the 5th houses (Taurus & Libra), the native may lose some children at an early age, and will be emotionally attached with the relatives of his family, helping them financially. But it will provide a good, thoughtful and artistic mate whose way of life would be different from him, creating occasional skirmishes with him.

## Saturn Transiting the Seventh House

When Saturn transits the seventh house, it makes the native cautious about all his relationships. It gives him a strong sense of responsibility and provides fairness in all his dealings with others. It is a good placement for working in the legal system or business management. It provides the individual a great sense of practicality with which he is able to solve his problems. It also tends to provide the native a matured mate who may be senior in age than him.

When Saturn owns the 1st and the 2nd houses (Capricorn & Aquarius) and is placed in the seventh house, it provides the native a scientific temperament. His mate is highly emotional and less attached to the family matters; his relationship with the mother is not quite normal. When Saturn owns the 3rd and the 4th houses (Capricorn & Aquarius), it makes the native judiciously communicative, develops an artistic bent of mind and helps to build a good house at 40 years of age. When it owns the 5th and the 6th houses (Capricorn & Aquarius), it may give a couple of sons, and a mate who is practical and attached to the family. When Saturn owns 7th and the 8th houses (Capricorn & Aquarius), it may give him a mate who is matured and senior to him in age but quite practical in household matters. The native is blessed with a long & healthy life.

*If Saturn owns the 9th and 10th houses (Capricorn & Aquarius) it makes the native lucky and brings him good luck at 45 years of age. He is in possession of good property, has a clever but short-tempered wife, and endowed with a good financial status. Officially he is involved with legal matters; he is farsighted, soft-spoken, loves music and enjoys working with his mates. When Saturn owns the 10th and 11th houses (Capricorn & Aquarius) and sits in the 7th house, it is one of the best placements financially and job-wise. Exalted Saturn in (Libra) the seventh house as the owner of the 10th and 11th houses provides the native a very attached and dutiful wife, gives a small number of progressive children, and a sudden financial benefit through his job at 46 years of age. Temperamentally he is artistic and romantic, loves music and dancing. At the same time he is not a puritan kind of person and believes in adjustments in life as it has debilitated aspects on the ascendant. If Mars, the owner of the ascendant, is well placed in the chart, it may develop the native's interest in technical areas also and help him earn money through legal work, teaching or business.*

When Saturn is placed in the seventh house and owns the 12th and the 1st houses (Capricorn & Aquarius), it makes him involved in various projects that require heavy investments of money. It provides a great desire to earn more and more money but as he is often involved in big projects that require big investments, his desire of earning does not get fulfilled. As Saturn has its aspects on the ascendant, it provides the native an extra sense of understanding and an insight with which he is able to handle his problems in his own way.

### *Rahu or Ketu Transiting the Seventh House*

When Rahu or Ketu transits the seventh house, it is not quite a wholesome placement as either of them provides unhappiness in married life. It brings either separation or unhappiness that comes on account of an unmanageable mate who is always demanding and pressurising the native in different ways. Unless the owner of the seventh house sits in a beneficial house or the seventh house has aspects from beneficial planets, the placement of Rahu or Ketu in the seventh house is not welcoming.

## Analysis of the Charts

Let us examine a few charts (*kundalis*) and discover how far the placements of different planets in the seventh house of the individuals working in different vocations affect them. We shall also like to identify certain *yogas,* adverse or favourable conjuncts in the seventh house that **cause delay, divorce or unhappiness in one's marriage.**

## Case Study One

The following chart belongs to an individual who graduated in hotel management and by the age of 45 years has changed several jobs. Let us examine how positive his 7th house has been to bring happiness in his life.

### Native born on 23rd June, 1961

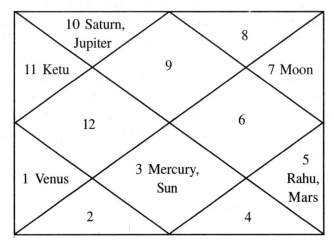

## Broad Analysis

Mercury as the owner of the 10th and 7th is conjunct in the 7th house with the Sun, owner of the 9th. It is a very good placement as far as the 7th house is concerned. It makes the native's seventh house pretty strong as the owner of the 7th Mercury is in its own sign and it aspects the ascendant along with the Sun, owner of the 9th house. Thus, both the owners of the 10th and the 9th houses have direct aspects on the ascendant, influencing it and providing it great strength. It leads to exert a lot of influence on the individual as far as the mate is concerned.

As there are no adverse influences on the 7th house from any malefic planets, the educated mate is contributing positively to the house of the native by running the whole show and by influencing the house by her own presence. In fact, native's life is absolutely influenced by her. Although she is highly educated and has not taken up any job except discharging household duties, she is recognised as a very important member of the house and whose opinion in every matter of the household is considered important.

*Thus, without any adverse influences on it, the 7th house makes the mate of the owner of the chart very important, responsible and able to contribute to the family in some way. Such combinations, conjuncts or influences lead to exert positive influences on the individual's life and the household as well. With such positive influences the native is likely to love her and abide by her opinions as she is greatly influential. The mate becomes more influential in a native's life when the ascendant of the native is weak in the chart as in the case of the above referred native whose ascendant Jupiter is placed in the 2nd house in a debilitated sign along with a strong Saturn.*

# Case Study Two

The following chart belongs to lady engineer born and settled in London.

## Native born on 27th October, 1967

```
┌─────────────────────────────────────────────┐
│  \           2          /  \   12 Saturn  /  │
│    \                  /      \          /     │
│  3   \              /          \      /       │
│        \    1 Rahu   \        /    11         │
│          \          /  \    /                 │
│    4 Moon  \      /      \ /      10          │
│          /   \  /        / \                  │
│        /      \ /      /     \                │
│ 5 Jupiter,  /  \  7 Sun,   /  \   9 Mars      │
│ Venus     /     \ Mercury,/     \             │
│          /       \ Ketu  /       \           │
│        /    6      \   /     8     \         │
└─────────────────────────────────────────────┘
```

## Broad Analysis

You can see various kinds of influences on the 7th house of the native and easily evaluate its strength. The placement of Rahu and Ketu in the 1st and the 7th respectively is a negative influence on the 7th as both these shadowy planets are bound to hurt the 7th house in some way although Ketu rises in the 7th in its friendly sign. Besides, a debilitated Sun in the 7th is also not an auspicious placement. Although it has an exalted aspect on the ascendant, it weakens the 7th house as it bestows an aggressive demeanour on the native. Besides, the ascendant, Mars, sitting in the 9th in its friendly sign makes the native's ascendant strong. It also tends to provide her quite an aggressive kind of demeanour that is detrimental in running family affairs smoothly. Not only that, Mars has aspects from Saturn as well as from a friendly Jupiter. It provides the native some sort of regimented behaviour, and also tender, intelligent as well as kind attitude in life.

Such factors influencing the native's demeanour also affect one's married life to a large extent. Besides, Venus, which is the natural owner of the 7$^{th}$, is conjunct with a strong Jupiter in the 5$^{th}$ house. It tends to provide her confusing ideas regarding marriage plans. As a result the native married once around 25 years of age (she has strong marriage *yogas* around 23, 25 and 29 years of her age) but soon after her marriage the alliance broke as Venus opposed by a strong Jupiter always created dislike towards her mate whom she herself chose perhaps in a hurry, being impulsive.

However, Mercury rising in a friendly sign in the 7$^{th}$ at the nativity will help her marry again. But she needs to keep in mind that any alliance made in a hurry and without matching the mate's chart could again be unfruitful. The best time of marriage for her could be immediately after 40 years, when Jupiter transits in its own sign (Sagittarius) after November, 2007.

*Thus, in order to assess the strength of the 7$^{th}$ house in a chart, one has to look for the benefic aspects on that house and see whether the owner of the 7$^{th}$ is well placed and rightly conjunct in the chart at the time of birth. A Venus-Jupiter alliance (conjunct), especially when Venus owns the 7$^{th}$ house, will surely be detrimental to the native in matrimonial matters.*

## Case Study Three

The following chart belongs to an America-based Indian doctor, born and educated in London, England. The native's parents are highly educated.

# Native born on 15ᵗʰ April, 1971

| | | |
|---|---|---|
| 1 Sun, Mercury, Saturn | 12 | 10 Rahu |
| 2 | 11 Venus | 9 Mars |
| 3 | 8 Jupiter, Moon | 7 |
| 4 Ketu | 5 | 6 |

*Chart layout:*

```
 1 Sun,        12              10 Rahu
 Mercury,
 Saturn            11 Venus               9 Mars

           2              8 Jupiter,
                          Moon

   3             5                  7

        4 Ketu               6
```

## Broad Analysis

The owner of the 7ᵗʰ, Sun, is sitting in the 3ʳᵈ house in the native's chart. As such, it predicts an early marriage approximately at the age of 27 but quite definitely at 29 years. Not only the owner of the 7ᵗʰ is exalted in the 3ʳᵈ house, it is also placed in the 9ᵗʰ from the 7ᵗʰ. It indicates quite an impulsive and amorous alliance with the partner whom the native is supposed to love very aggressively. Mercury as the owner of the 5ᵗʰ is conjunct with the owner of the 7ᵗʰ, which also indicates emotional and early alliance with an educated mate.

Debilitated Saturn, sitting in the 3ʳᵈ house, conjuncts with the Sun, which is its natural enemy. It predicts some problems in the marriage, especially when Saturn transits in Libra after four and a half years from now (2007). As a strong Venus has aspects on the 7ᵗʰ house from the ascendant, it works as an oasis in the married life of the native. Yet no other positive influence on the 7ᵗʰ house indicates differences and problems in the marriage of the native. As quickly as the marriage took place and the native was indulged in the romantic deal with the mate belonging to a different country, relations might break with the same speed except that children could hold the alliance for some time.

Again, an exalted Sun being the owner of the 7th sitting with Saturn will always create problems for the native. The mate is supposed to be bossy, impulsive and not agreeable in most of the matters with the native. It is going to happen because the native's ascendant is Saturn that is in a debilitated sign and the owner of the 7th Sun is in an exalted sign. Both are conjunct in the 3rd house which is quite a strong house from the point of view of the 7th as well as the ascendant (1st house). Planets attain strength when they are placed in the 9th house from their ownership. Besides, Saturn in the 3rd house from its own sign is also considered strong. As such, detrimental results of the alliance are bound to take place especially after four and a half years from now (2007) when Saturn transits in Libra and aspects Mars, Sun and the sixth house.

*Therefore, to assess the strength of the 7th house, it is important to see what sign is occupied by its owner and in what house it is placed in the chart at the time of the native's birth. Besides, it is also necessary to observe that neither the owner of the 7th nor the 7th house should have aspects or be conjunct with the malefic planets. Such aspects or conjuncts are likely to sour the native's relationship with the mate, especially when malefic planets have aspects on the 7th or the owner of the 7th house.*

## Case Study Four

The following chart belongs to a law graduate and MBA from USA, and who holds a very high position in Reliance (a leading telecom company). He is a leading lawyer in the town. He is very strong financially and has acquired great respect among his people at an early age.

## Native born on 10ᵗʰ July, 1975

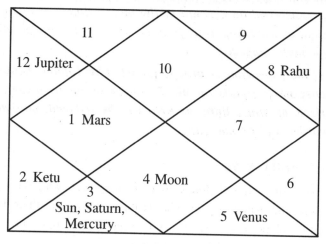

## Broad Analysis

The Moon, the owner of the 7ᵗʰ, is sitting in its own sign in that house. As such, it provides a very charming and caring wife who should always remain attached with the native. The seventh house Moon placed in its own sign has positive aspects from Jupiter, its natural friend. It further provides strength to the 7ᵗʰ house. Mars, the owner of the 4ᵗʰ and 11ᵗʰ also aspects the Moon, which makes the native's chart *manglik*.

That simply means that it possesses Mars' ill aspects (*drishti-dosha*) on it. It could lead to separation from the mate, or a divorce or death to the partner. Consequently, the native's beloved wife died after a couple of years of their marriage. But as the 7ᵗʰ house has very benefic aspects from Jupiter (exalted aspects) the native remarried within a year's time from the death of his first wife. They both are living happily after the marriage.

*It must be clear to the reader that Mars' aspects on the 7ᵗʰ house are bound to bring bad effects on that house and consequently, the married life of the mate may be adversely affected in any of the following ways: There may be divorce during Mars' dasha (period) or antar-dasha (sub-period), or the native may have a very difficult time as far as married life is concerned on account of the mate's illness, diversity of attention or travelling away from the town causing separation, or the mate may die.*

*At the same time if benefic planets like Jupiter, Venus or Mercury have aspects on the 7th house or on its owner, the ill effects of Mars, Rahu or Ketu can be reduced, minimised or warded off permanently.*

## Case Study Five

The following chart belongs to a businessman who has more than ten established private schools throughout Rajasthan. He is friendly and possesses riches and property that have provided him respect and great social status.

### Native born on 5th December, 1967

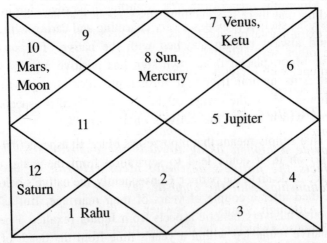

### Broad Analysis

The owner of the 7th, Venus, is sitting in the 12th conjunct with Ketu. Tradition unfolds that Venus in the 12th in its own sign is not detrimental to the native and may provide him with the company of a caring mate, though of independent nature and a spendthrift as well. At the same time the owners of the 10th and

11$^{th}$, the Sun and Mercury, are conjunct at the ascendant and have aspects on the 7$^{th}$. That also provides an artistic leaning and finer taste in the mate. Saturn's aspects on the 7$^{th}$ also need to be considered to ascertain the strength of the 7$^{th}$. In fact, Saturn's aspects on the 7$^{th}$ are not considered very favourable. Yet in the above chart the 7$^{th}$ house belongs to Saturn's natural friend, Venus. Therefore, it would not harm that house. Instead, it is expected that it may provide artistic tastes and conversational abilities in the mate.

As the Sun and Mercury occupy the ascendant, the native is involved with teaching business. He has a chain of schools at different places and big towns in the state of Rajasthan, collecting good revenue through that business. Besides, an exalted Mars in the 3$^{rd}$ also makes him highly effortful, friendly, and determined. All these qualities are also good for the kind of business he is involved in. But his 7$^{th}$ house having aspects from Mercury, Sun and Saturn and its owner Venus sitting in the 12$^{th}$ provide an inkling that there is something fussy about that house. It shows his extra-marital relationship as well as his constant leaning towards the other sex, although the Sun sitting at the ascendant and conjunct with Mercury does not clearly permit him to indulge in such activities.

*Therefore, let us keep in mind that different kinds of aspects on the 7$^{th}$ house from the planets of opposite nature provide a hidden liking towards the opposite sex. It also affects the native's aesthetic ideas relating to sex and relationships with the opposite sex.*

Although Venus, the owner of the 7$^{th}$ is sitting in the 12$^{th}$ house, (which is the 6$^{th}$ house from the 7$^{th}$) it may not delay the marriage of the native. But it could often happen if other planets having ownership of the 7$^{th}$ are placed in the 12$^{th}$ house. We shall refer in this section certain cases of the natives in whose charts either Jupiter or Saturn being the owner of the 7$^{th}$ are sitting in the 12$^{th}$ house and have caused concerning delays in their marriages.

# Case Study Six

The following chart belongs to a Bangalore-based young man who is struggling hard to keep himself up in the SiliconValley of India, trying to avert his marriage for some time until he is nicely settled in life.

**Native born on 5ᵗʰ October, 1982**

## Broad Analysis

When we examine the 7ᵗʰ house of the native, we find that its owner Sun is placed in the 8ᵗʰ house and is conjunct with Mercury, Venus and Saturn. It is really not so bad for a planet to sit in the next house from its ownership, but it being conjunct with malefic planets may be detrimental to the native. The Sun and Saturn are natural enemies to each other. Therefore, the 7ᵗʰ house of the native is adversely affected and has been providing him different kinds of ideas regarding his marriage. He has been doggedly refusing to accept marriage proposals until recently when Saturn entered in Leo sign from November 2006. Fortunately, the 7ᵗʰ house itself has no ill aspects, but its owner is conjunct with Saturn that is equally unfavourable for the native as far as his marriage is concerned. Until good aspects from beneficial planets are experienced by that house, the native cannot decide to go for his marriage. When Saturn transited in Leo in November 2006, and stopped having aspects on the Sun from Cancer in which it transited for almost two and half years before November 2006, that he has started giving a serious thought to marry.

The owner of the 5th, Mercury, is well placed and is in its exalted sign. It is conjunct in the 8th house with Saturn and Venus, which are its natural friends. Consequently, the native has been accepting projects and time-bound jobs in Bangalore to pull himself on. The most favourable planet in the native's chart is Mars, which is sitting in its own sign in the 10th house. It makes the native highly effortful, self-reliant and attached to his father. Because of that he has been accepting even smaller jobs far from his hometown, just to carry on his studies and helping his father and family.

Well, these matters are not directly related to the 7th house, but to some extent there is certain relationship with it. The native, being very effortful and responsible towards his family, has not been accepting marriage proposals in order to help every one of them. Again, the owner of the *lagna*, (ascendant) and the owner of the 7th are not natural friends. It has also affected his marriage plans that we have already briefly discussed above. The best period of accepting the marriage proposals starts after November 2007, when Jupiter transits in Sagittarius and aspects the 3rd, the 5th and the 7th houses. The owner of the 7th house being the Sun, which is Jupiter's natural friend, will highly facilitate by Jupiter's aspects and certainly tie the native in matrimonial alliances.

*Therefore, one must keep in mind that any kind of influence or aspect of Saturn on its enemy house (having Leo sign), which if happens to be the 7th house in a chart, is bound to bring adverse results to the native. It can lead to delay or disruption in the marriage, or may bring disharmony or separation.*

# Case Study Seven

The following chart belongs to a gynaecologist who is married to an educated lady fruitfully employed as a teacher in a State Government set-up.

## Native born on 4ᵗʰ February, 1959

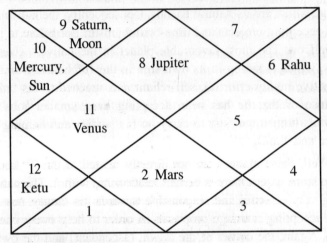

## Broad Analysis

The above chart is a clear example of a good 7ᵗʰ house as its owner, Venus, is well placed in the chart. Not only that but Jupiter, the owner of the 5ᵗʰ and the 2ⁿᵈ houses, also aspects Mars which is the owner of the ascendant and sits in the 7ᵗʰ house. Jupiter's aspect on the 7ᵗʰ and Mars being its natural friend have mutual aspects on each other from the 1ˢᵗ and the 7ᵗʰ houses. It provides the 7ᵗʰ house considerable strength and promises the native a devoted and caring wife. Although Mars sitting in the 7ᵗʰ does create some kind of *dosha* (*manglik*) that inflicts some kind of harm to the 7ᵗʰ house, but as it is the owner of the ascendant and has aspects from Jupiter, that *dosha* is cancelled. If we examine the native's chart very carefully we also observe Saturn's aspects on Venus, the owner of the 7ᵗʰ house. It makes the native's partner less aggressive and provides her a certain kind of judicious inkling with which she can always extend sane advice to her partner since she is a more practical kind of person.

Again, Venus is sitting in the 10th from the 7th, which happens to be the 4th house in the native's chart and strengthens the 7th house as Venus is not only one sign ahead (Aquarius) of its exalted sign (*ucchabhilashi*), its placement is also very auspicious as it is rising in its friend's sign. It also indicates a very caring and devoted wife, who is educated, responsible, possessed with artistic qualities and well versed in the household matters. Most of the house or property-related matters are going to be pushed by her as the owner of the 7th is rising in the 4th house.

*It is, therefore, necessary for the reader to keep in mind that good aspects on the seventh or its placement in an auspicious house or sign are bound to provide very good results making the native and his family happy. The mate will not only support the native in all matters in life, but will also willingly help him in household and property-related matters.*

## Case Study Eight

The following chart belongs to a lady computer engineer who is about to complete her MBA from a reputed college in the country. When this chart is being examined (March 2007), she is interviewed for a good job and promised to be hired by a reputed company.

### Native born on 16th May, 1983

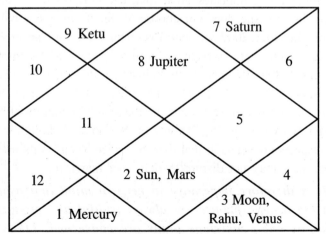

## Broad Analysis

The above chart belongs to an individual born almost 24 years after the person whose chart we have discussed under **Case Study Seven** in this section of the book. You can see Jupiter rising at the ascendant and Mars also placed in the 7th house. But the owner of the 7th, Venus, is placed in the 8th house conjunct with the Moon and Rahu. Besides, the owner of the 10th, Sun, is also conjunct with Mars in the 7th house. All such aspects, conjuncts and placements have influenced the 7th house of the native in different ways. Let us analyse all that.

Jupiter and Mars have mutual aspects on each other and provide the native opportunity to fall in love with someone at an early age. It is just the placement of the Sun conjunct with Mars that has affected primarily the marriage plans of the native. The Sun-Mars conjunct in the 7th delays the native's marriage plans as the Sun being the owner of the 10th infuses in the native the desire to work and to stay as a career person. Besides, Venus' conjunct with the Moon in the 8th is also instrumental in delaying the native's marriage plans as Venus is also the owner of the 12th house and sits in the 8th, which is not quite an auspicious house traditionally. However, Jupiter's transits in the sign Scorpio and having aspects on the 5th, 7th and the 9th houses until November 2007, indicates good marriage opportunities for the native. In case she does not choose to decide to marry by the end of May-June 2007, as Saturn is retrograding in Cancer until mid-July 2007, her marriage plans may be delayed for another two years (2009-10) when Jupiter will transit in the sign Capricorn and aspect the 7th, 9th and the 11th houses. By December 2009 (approx), Saturn will start transiting the sign Virgo and will have no adverse aspects on the 7th house of the native. Although it will have aspects on Venus at that time but since Venus is its natural friend, so it may not disrupt or delay her marriage.

*It is therefore imperative to keep in mind that aspects from the benefic planets are always fruitful and productive as far as one's marriage plans are concerned. Likewise, aspects from the malefic planets on the 7ᵗʰ house, including Rahu and Ketu, certainly cause delay and disruption in marriages unless in both the charts (of male and female) similar kinds of yogas or aspects exist that may cancel the ill effects of the aspects of the malefic planets.*

## Case Study Nine

The following chart belongs to a young man who is currently working in his own home organisation relating to car services. His marriage is delayed on account of various flimsy reasons.

### Native born on 12ᵗʰ January, 1980

| | | |
|---|---|---|
| 7 Moon | | 5 Jupiter, Mars, Rahu |
| 8 | 6 Saturn | 4 |
| 9 Sun, Mercury | | 3 |
| 10 | 12 | 2 |
| 11 Venus, Ketu | 1 | |

## *Broad Analysis*

The owner of the 7ᵗʰ, Jupiter, *yogakarak* for marriage, is rising in the 12ᵗʰ house (6ᵗʰ from the 7ᵗʰ house) and is conjunct with Ketu and Mars, which are detrimental for the marriage or for the 7ᵗʰ house. Besides, Saturn has its aspects on the 7ᵗʰ from the ascendant. Mars also has its adverse aspect on the 7ᵗʰ house forming a *manglik yoga*. All these adverse aspects and the owner of the 7ᵗʰ Jupiter rising in 12ᵗʰ house are causing delay in the native's marriage. He often rejects the photographs of the girls saying that he does not like the girl. Once or twice he has visited a couple of girls personally, but without any positive results. He is already 27 years old when his chart is being analysed (March 2007). Most of the members in the family are concerned about his marriage although he hasn't grown too old. Even after constant efforts for seeking a suitable match for him, all efforts have been futile so far. We reckon the simple reason for delay in his marriage is on account of the owner of the 7th, Jupiter, is sitting in the 12th from where it cannot exert any positive influence on the 7th house. Besides, Saturn and Mars also have aspects on that house causing delay in the marriage plans.

*Therefore, one should keep in mind that unless the owner of the 7th is not fruitfully or favourably placed at the time of the birth, marriage of a native is likely to be delayed or postponed. Besides, Saturn's and Mars' aspects on the 7th house also delays or disrupts one's marriage.*

The best years for the native's marriage could be between November 2007 to November 2008, and even one year after it, when Jupiter transits in the most favourable signs (Scorpio and Sagittarius), and will have aspects on the 7th house and its owner respectively.

## Case Study Ten

The following chart belongs to a lady doctor who is a lecturer in a reputable medical college established in the western part of India. The doctor is married and has been living with her husband who is unconcerned, only to help her two children grow well for she cares too much for them.

## Native born on 27th June, 1969

```
┌─────────────────────────────────────────────┐
│ \           3 Sun        /  1 Saturn,    \   │
│   \                    /      Venus        \ │
│     \                /                       │
│  4    \            /   2 Mercury    \   12 Rahu│
│         \        /                    \      │
│           \    /                        \    │
│      5      \/            11             /    │
│             /\                         /      │
│           /    \                     /        │
│ 6 Ketu, /        \   8 Mars,       /          │
│ Jupiter           \   Moon       /    10      │
│       \    7       \           / 9            │
└─────────────────────────────────────────────┘
```

## Broad Analysis

She was married when around 27 years of age and in a couple of years she gave birth to two children. But soon the debilitated Moon conjunct with a strong Mars in the 7th house started creating problems in her married life. It is on account of her traditional way of thinking (Mercury rising at the ascendant) and caring for the public opinion (the owner of 11th Jupiter, having aspects on the 11th) that she has not formally taken a divorce from her husband, otherwise she would have been separated from him around 8 years back (from now i.e. 2007) when Saturn was transiting the sign Taurus.

In fact, the Moon rising in a debilitated sign in the 7th house could become a cause of skirmishes and lead to unhappy alliance. Besides, Mars, though rising in its own sign in the 7th, may also cause disruption in the marriage. There is one more factor that needs to be considered seriously when finding out one's happiness in marriage. It is the placement of Venus in a native's chart and the sign in which Venus rises. Although Venus placed in the 12th house is not considered inauspicious, it may not bestow favourable results placed in the signs not belonging to its natural friends. Besides, Venus conjunct with Saturn in the 12th house can inflict more harm to a native than any benefits as it cultivates frigidity in the individual. As a frigid person cannot fulfil the partner's needs easily, it might become a cause of disruption of relationship, mainly when the other partner is more demanding. Some of these reasons would have led to weakening the relationship with her husband. However, an exalted aspect on the ascendant from the Moon is also helpful in keeping the thread intact to a certain extent. Even if the relationship has become weak, occasional intimate meetings would surely go on to keep them living together.

*Once again the reader needs to keep in mind that malefic aspects or conjunct at the 7th could lead to disruption of married relationship. Besides the adverse role of Saturn, a strong Mars is often instrumental in weakening relationships in marriages.*

## Case Study Eleven

The following chart belongs to an American lady who is working as a private medical practitioner in hospitals and has married a person of a different country and caste. She works as per her own choice and visits hospitals at her convenience.

### Native born on 30th July, 1968

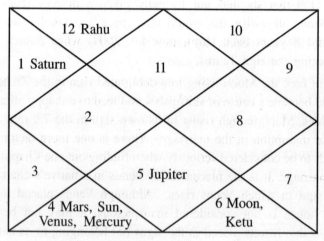

## Broad Analysis

The native is born when Aquarius is rising at the ascendant. The owner of the ascendant and the 12th house, Saturn, is rising in its debilitated sign in the 3rd house, which makes her lethargic, less effortful, involving in fruitless errands, and highly choosy about her friends. When we examine the strength of her 7th house we find a strong Jupiter rising in the sign Leo in that house. It provides a lot of strength to 7th house and to the ascendant as well. Jupiter, being the owner of the 11th and 2nd houses — both being related to riches and finances respectively, is highly beneficial to the native as far as her financial gains from her husband are concerned. Besides, Jupiter aspects the 1st, the 3rd (debilitated Saturn) and the 11th houses. It provides her some agility to work and to stay sane although Saturn rising in a debilitation sign in the 3rd house (being the owner of the 1st and 12th houses) is often likely to provide the native low ideas towards work, friends and relatives. However, Jupiter's strong aspects on the ascendant as well as on the owner of the ascendant cancels most of such weak *yogas*. Jupiter has also helped her to continue with her partner in spite of having stormy weather many a time.

The Sun, owner of the 7th, is sitting in the 12th house from its ownership. Besides it is also conjunct with Mars that can weaken the married relationship. Again, Mars, that is the owner of 10th and 3rd houses, is rising in the 6th house in its debilitation sign. It may not permit the native to be effortful in a focussed manner and often may also lead her to waste efforts. But Mars being the controller of medical science, and is also the owner of the 10th, has led the native to work in the medical field. Since most of the planets in the lady's chart are rising in the 6th house, which is not a very beneficial house as far as traditional astrology is concerned, the native may often involve herself in antagonism, wasteful efforts for want of right direction, and be less productive. But she will always be gaining from her husband as Jupiter is well placed in the 7th house. It will help to eradicate the bad effects of other planets to a large extent as it (Jupiter) has benefic aspects on the ascendant.

*The reader must keep in mind that if beneficial planets are rising in the 7th house or it (7th house) has aspects from the yogakarak planets, the native is bound to receive benefits from the mate even though the ascendant or the Moon or the owner of the 10th is not well placed in a chart.*

## Case Study Twelve

The following chart belongs to a senior lecturer working in an established College of Education for the last ten years and earns good reputation as a teacher of his subject. He is a hard working and painstaking teacher who is always willing to help his students.

### Native born on 4th April, 1965

*Broad Analysis*

When we examine the 7th house of the native, we find different kinds of ill aspects on it. Not only that, a strong Saturn is rising in the 7th house, Mars also has its aspects on the 7th house and its owner, leaving very small chances to have a happy married life. Mars not only aspects the 7th house and its owner, it also aspects the owner of the ascendant, which further affects his married relationship. Consequently, immediately after his marriage in a week's time the mate separated from the native on flimsy grounds. Later on, relationship was further severed, forcing him to go for a divorce. All that happened in a few months after the marriage. It was obviously a very painful experience, more because the native declined to remarry as his personal responsibilities towards his family are immense.

If we further examine the chart we find no benefic aspect on the 7th house. Therefore, the native seems to have made up his mind not to marry in future. It is a hurting situation to the family as the native is the eldest child. In fact, there is not much to discuss about the native's chart from the point of view of the 7th house or a happy married life.

*Mars' aspects on the owner of the 7th and the 7th house as well, including its aspects on the Sun which is the ascendant (sitting in the 8th house), has adversely affected the 7th house of the native.* Except that if ever he comes in contact with someone in whose chart the 7th house is also badly afflicted, marriage or friendship can take place again.

## Case Study Thirteen

The following chart belongs to the son of a successful businessman involved in wholesale and retail selling of cloth. His family is involved with that kind of business for four generations capturing the local market very successfully in a small district in the western part of India.

**Native born on 30th November, 1964**

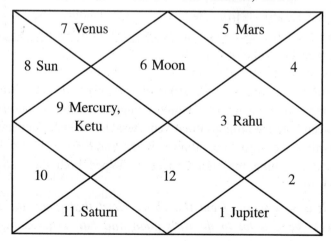

## Broad Analysis

When we examine the native's chart carefully, we observe that Jupiter, the owner of the 7<sup>th</sup> house, is rising in Aries in the 8<sup>th</sup> house. The seventh house has benefic aspects from the Moon, which owns the 11<sup>th</sup> and is rising at the ascendant. These two good factors led the native to marry someone whom he liked to a great extent. But there are two adverse aspects on the 7<sup>th</sup> and the owner of the 7<sup>th</sup> too. Mars, which is rising in the 12<sup>th</sup> house, has adverse aspects (*manglik*) on the 7<sup>th</sup> house. Besides, Venus is rising in the 2<sup>nd</sup> house and aspects Jupiter from there. Venus and Jupiter being natural enemies to each other are bound to create disruption in the native's married life bringing them to the brink of divorce and often ill health to the mate. When Saturn was transiting the sign Gemini (2002-2005) and had aspects on the 7<sup>th</sup> house, the families of the native and the mate filed a petition in the court of law against each other requesting grant of divorce. But as soon as Saturn entered in the sign Cancer and stopped its aspects on the 7<sup>th</sup> house, gradually, both the parties compromised. The girl started living with her husband (native) who too did not really want to take a divorce from her. Why did all that happen, with both the families spending lots of money in the court procedures? The only answer is that the adverse aspects from Saturn and Mars on the 7<sup>th</sup> led to that sort of disruption. But benefic aspects from the Moon (on the 7<sup>th</sup> house) and Jupiter's aspects on the ascendant Mercury are good enough to help continue that relationship. Although Venus aspects Jupiter that leads to create emotional and health problems to the mate, they are still continuing. When Saturn switched over to the sign Cancer, it stopped looking at the 7<sup>th</sup> house. Gradually the bad relationship between both the families improved. Besides, when Jupiter started transiting the sign Leo, almost at the same time Saturn also started transiting the sign Cancer. It helped both the families patch up.

*It is so obvious from the above chart that good and bad aspects have a lot to do with good and bad relationship in one's married life. Especially, when Saturn and Mars have adverse aspects on the 7th house disruption in the married life is bound to happen. Saturn's aspects on Jupiter (owner of the 7th) did not harm the native's married life, as Saturn and Jupiter are not natural enemies traditionally. Still, Venus having its aspect on Jupiter often keeps the mate indisposed. Consequently, their married life gets disturbed from time to time. Yet the good aspects are constantly keeping them on for good.*

## Case Study Fourteen

The following chart belongs to the daughter of a jeweller who deals in precious stones and gold ornaments. She has obtained a post-graduate degree in humanities and is working in a local company, waiting to get married. The parents are extremely concerned about her marriage, as she has completed 26 years in June 2007.

**Native born on 10th June, 1981**

```
            4 Rahu              2 Mars, Sun
     5            3 Mercury,            1
                     Venus
        6 Jupiter,
       Moon, Saturn          12
     7              9               11
           8              10 Ketu
```

## Broad Analysis

When we examine the above chart carefully, we find Mars' adverse aspects on the 7th house. Mars is rising in the 12th house making a *manglik yoga*. We have already examined a couple of charts in this section with that kind of *yoga* when Mars exerts its malefic aspects on the 7th house causing delay or some kind of disruption in the native's married life. Saturn's transit in the sign Cancer since the last quarter of 2004 (until November 2007), has caused delay in the marriage. During this period Saturn has aspects on Jupiter which is the owner of the 7th house. Although Saturn is not a permanent enemy of Jupiter traditionally, it has landed a helping hand to Mars in delaying the marriage.

After November 2007 Jupiter will transit the sign Sagittarius and will have positive aspects on the ascendant Mercury, and will transit in the 7th house. It may help the native to fulfil her desires. Besides, Jupiter transiting in its own sign Sagittarius being the owner of the 7th, will be *yogakarak* for the native's marriage.

*Once again Mars' adverse aspects on the 7th house have caused some delay in the marriage of the native. Besides, good aspects of Jupiter when it transits in a favourable sign are also likely to exert positive influence on the 7th house bestowing happiness to the native by fulfilling her dreams.*

## Brief Summary of Results

*If the Sun sits in the seventh and owns the 9th house, it is a great placement as it owns the house of luck. It helps the native through the spouse, who is often caring and loving, and supports the native financially as well as in social and family matters. If the Sun owns the 10th house and sits in the seventh, it may cultivate artistic qualities and gives a very caring and loving partner. When the Sun owns the 11th house and sits in the 7th house, it helps financially through the spouse and makes the native popular and socially respected.*

*When Jupiter owns the 1st & 4th houses (Sagittarius & Pisces) and is placed in the 7th house, it provides the native a charming personality and people respect him as he is honest and straightforward. His relationship with his mother is good and he is the owner of a good house often provided by his parents. The spouse is highly educated, supportive and loving. His communicative capabilities, both in speech and writing, are often praiseworthy.*

*When Saturn owns the 10<sup>th</sup> and 11<sup>th</sup> houses (Capricorn & Aquarius) and sits in the 7<sup>th</sup> house (Libra), it is one of the best placements financially and job-wise. It also provides the native a very caring and dutiful wife, gives a couple of good and progressive children, and a sudden financial benefit through his job at 46 years of age.*

*Mars' aspects on the owner of the 7<sup>th</sup> and the 7<sup>th</sup> house as well, including its aspects on the ascendant sitting in the 8<sup>th</sup> house, may adversely affect the 7<sup>th</sup> house of the native, leaving small chances to have a good and happy married life.*

*It is so obvious from the above examples given in this section of the book that good and bad aspects on the 7<sup>th</sup> house and its owner have to do a lot with good and bad relationship in one's married life. When Saturn and Mars have adverse aspects on the 7<sup>th</sup> house, disruption in the married life is bound to happen. But Saturn's aspects on Jupiter (when it owns the 7<sup>th</sup> house) may not bring much harm to the native's smooth running married life, as Saturn and Jupiter are not natural enemies traditionally. Still, Venus having its aspect on Jupiter (if it is the ruler of the 7<sup>th</sup> house) often keeps the mate indisposed or emotionally less tuned. Consequently, one's married life gets disturbed from time to time due to different reasons.*

## When Matching Charts for Marriage!

In this section of the book we shall provide certain useful hints to the reader regarding matching charts prior to marriage. In fact, it is absolutely impossible to match two charts perfectly accurate and it is also true that when two persons of opposite sex hailing from different family environments get united, certain problems are bound to occur. But as an astrologer you have to keep in view the following points so that you may suggest whether the two charts are well matched and the married life of the two to be joined as husband and wife would be happy and productive.

1. We reckon the signs, ownerships and placements of the ascendant and the owner of the 7th houses are the first to be taken into consideration. If these two are well placed, are rising in friendly signs as well as rule good houses, the *kundalis* could be accepted to be united.

2. There should not be any adverse aspects on the 7th from the owners of the 12th, Mars and Saturn including Rahu & Ketu, for such aspects are likely to bring unhappiness and disruption in the marriage.

3. As far as possible the match maker (astrologer) must possess the knowledge to read from reputed Hindi/Sanskrit *Panchang* (calendar that contains material relating to the planets' day to day movements and also reflects how to calculate the total *gunas* formed by the *nakshatras* owned by the moon signs in the man and woman's chart) and find out the total number of *gunas*. If such *gunas* thus calculated are less than 18, as far as possible, final acceptance may not be given. If it is absolutely necessary to go for the marriage on account of social or family reasons, then the astrologer must assess the strength of the ascendant, the 7th house, and also of the 5th house. If the owners of these houses, especially the ascendant and the 7th house are well placed or are rising in their friendly sign and don't have aspects from Saturn or Mars, charts could be accepted for marriage.

4. As far as possible two charts, when matched, must not have aspects from Mars or Saturn or Rahu and Ketu on the 7th house. (See chart no. Twelve) But in case both the charts have such aspects, *kundalis* can be accepted.

5. It is absolutely necessary that the owner of the 7th should be placed in a beneficial house and should not be rising in

the 12$^{th}$ house (six from 7$^{th}$) or the 2$^{nd}$ house (eighth from the 7$^{th}$) at the time of birth. Such placement certainly delays or disrupts the marriages. (See chart no. Eight given in this section)

6. However, the best decision to accept or to reject two charts or *kundalis* should depend on favourably placed 7$^{th}$ house-owner. If the 7$^{th}$ house or its owner has aspects from Jupiter, there is a pretty good chance to lead a happy married life. (See chart no. Ten)

7. If two charts are simply united on the basis of the strength of the *gunas* only without considering the strength of the owners of the ascendant and the 7$^{th}$ houses, it may lead to disruption or divorce in the marriage.

8. Exchange of the owners of the ascendant and the 7$^{th}$ house in friendly signs is a good sign of a happy marriage. However, if such exchanges occur, when Jupiter or Venus rules 1$^{st}$ or 7$^{th}$, or 7$^{th}$ or 1$^{st}$ houses, it should not be approved for it is going to bring unhappiness in the married life.

9. When Jupiter transits in its own sign or in a friendly sign in a chart and aspects the 7$^{th}$ house or its owner, then even though the owner of the 7$^{th}$ is sitting in the 12$^{th}$ or 2$^{nd}$ houses in the *kundali* (chart), it should be taken very auspicious to match a *kundali* and to approve the marriage in an auspicious month when the Sun is not adversely transiting in that chart.

10. It is believed that if Mars rises in its own sign or friendly sign in the 7$^{th}$ house, it does not disturb the native's married life. We hold that Mars' aspects on the 7$^{th}$ house either from 12$^{th}$, 4$^{th}$ or 7$^{th}$ houses are bound to exert adverse effects on a native's married life even if it rises in a friendly sign in a chart. Can there be a better example than Sri Ram's *kundali* in which an exalted Mars is rising in the 7$^{th}$ house even if an exalted Jupiter transits at the ascendant?

# The Eleventh House
### House of Idealism, Dreams and Riches

**W**estern astrologers hold that the eleventh house deals with friends, hopes, wishes, long-term dreams and goals. It is the house where you find your sense of future direction and purpose of life. The eleventh house relates to your idealism and dreams for the collective good of the people, for attaining social goals, reforms and need to contribute towards people's happiness and welfare. It is the house that deals with the accomplishments of your ideals, aspirations for the benefit of the people of your community and country.

Indian astrological traditions consider this house related to your life's gains, your financial status, gains through your parents, ancestors, and sudden and unexpected riches you may have in life. In fact, the second house, which indicates your hard earned incomes and financial benefits, is complementary to the eleventh house. If the owners of both, the second and the eleventh houses, are well placed in a chart, they certainly indicate great wealth and riches in one's life. Let us examine each planet's ownership through different houses when it transits the eleventh house.

# Transits of Planets

When planets occupy the eleventh house and own a beneficial house they enhance the strength of both the houses—the eleventh as well as the house they own. Let us evaluate the transits of the planets including the nodes, Rahu and Ketu, and find out their effect on individuals' lives.

## Sun Transiting the Eleventh House

When the Sun transits the eleventh house it often makes an individual popular, rich, creative, possessing a will power that helps continue social order. If the Sun is placed in the eleventh house, the subject has a desire to accomplish something important that may benefit others. Such a subject often possesses humanitarian goals in life, with which he is prepared to improve others' lives. He is always ready to help the needy and the downtrodden.

*When the Sun occupies the eleventh house and owns the $1^{st}$ house, it makes the individual very rich and socially popular. The individual has the benefit of regular money inflow and hardly suffers from lack of money. When the Sun owns the $2^{nd}$ house and sits in the eleventh, it provides benefits through artistic talents. He is respected by his own people and makes him very rich. When it owns the $3^{rd}$ house it makes the subject highly effortful, dynamic, very hard working, honest and dashing. He possesses influential brothers and friends.*

When the Sun owns the $4^{th}$ house and sits in the eleventh, it provides great property and love from mother. When it owns the $5^{th}$ house, it gives a couple of bright sons who assist him in life. He is always respected by his community. When the Sun owns the $6^{th}$ house and sits in the $11^{th}$ house, the subject may have some problems from his sons, enemies and his partners. When it owns the $7^{th}$ house, it helps the native financially through his mate who is matured enough to stay with him in different walks of life. When the Sun owns the $8^{th}$ house and sits in the eleventh, it provides the native great physical strength and a strong will power. When the Sun owns the 9th house, it provides the native at least one son who excels in life in status and finances and stays with him in spite of some differences with him.

*When the Sun owns the 10th or 11th house and sits in the eleventh, it always provides financial benefits from business and government and the native gets great respect from the people and the community he lives with. It is a great placement of the Sun.*

When it owns the 12th house and sits in the eleventh, it is not a wholesome placement as it leads to loss of money and prestige, and keeps the native constantly worried on account of personal problems created by children and friends as well.

## Moon Transiting the Eleventh House

When the Moon transits the eleventh house, it makes the native emotionally attached with the people of his community and provides riches and gains from parents, especially mother. The individual possesses emotional attachment for the greater good of the people and is always ready to help the needy.

*When the Moon transits the eleventh house and owns the 1st house, the individual is always well off financially and gets respect from people of his community. He is highly emotional and attached to his family and mother. When it occupies the eleventh and rules the 2nd house, financially it is one of the best placements of the Moon.*

When the Moon is the lord of the 3rd house and sits in the eleventh, it provides more number of sisters and more female friends who are attached to the native and ready to help him. While putting efforts he is inclined to work more, and is emotionally backed up by his feelings. When the Moon rules the 4th house it benefits the native with mother's care and love and provides him benefits from the property given by either of the parents, especially by the mother. When the Moon owns the 5th house and sits in the eleventh, it gives more number of daughters, makes the individual highly imaginative and inclines him to write poetry. When it owns the 6th house and sits in the eleventh, it is not quite a healthy sign as it may, from time to time, give the native social problems, disharmony through partners but occasional gains from legal matters. When the Moon owns the 7th house and sits in the eleventh house, it predicts financial benefits from a quarrelsome and fault finding spouse, gives some kind of social problems on account of sharp tongue of the native. When the Moon owns the 8th house and sits in the eleventh, it may give one good looking son and more daughters, and may provide occasional financial help from relatives, and benefit the native with certain amount of social prestige. When it owns the 9th house and sits in the eleventh, it is quite a good placement as it may give a charming partner, good luck at the age of 22 years and social acclaim by the people.

*When the Moon owns the 10th or 11th house and sits in the eleventh, it certainly provides benefits through good jobs and high placements in life. The native may choose water-related jobs as careers in life and may get high respect from his community and women especially.*

When the Moon owns the 12th house and sits in the eleventh, it makes the person a spendthrift, mostly misunderstood, financially weak but constantly possessing an increased lust for money and property.

## Mars Transiting the Eleventh House

It is quite a good placement provided Mars also rules a good sign or a beneficial house in the chart. Such a native is often a leader in his friends circle. He pursues the goals of his life very actively. The native is capable to make new friends very quickly and may turn into a revolutionary if he is dissatisfied with the present circumstances. Mars' placement in the 11th house also gives riches and social prestige.

*When Mars owns the 1ˢᵗ and the 8ᵗʰ houses (Aries & Scorpio) and sits in the 11ᵗʰ, it is a highly beneficial position as it provides good status and gives financial benefits. It also provides the native good health and extra energy to work and a great capacity to look after his business interests. It also provides good job opportunities in medical or police fields.*

When Mars owns the 2ⁿᵈ and the 9ᵗʰ houses (Aries & Scorpio) and is placed in the eleventh house, it gives good luck around 28 years of age. The subject has great social popularity though he possesses an unbending outlook and conduct. He earns a great deal in life through hard work and stroke of good luck, which will always support him in life. He may have some kind of problems relating to children. He may have only one son who may be born after he is 29 or 30 years old, or the son may remain indisposed quite occasionally until he has reached eleven years of age.

*When Mars owns the 3ʳᵈ and the 10ᵗʰ houses (Aries & Scorpio) it provides great riches through medical-related fields; if the owner of the 7ᵗʰ house, Sun, is also well placed in the chart of a native, it gives a caring and loving wife who also helps him financially, provided it (seventh house owner) is placed in the eleventh or the third house. Such a placement makes the subject highly communicative and socially well placed too. When Mars owns the 4ᵗʰ and the 11ᵗʰ houses (Aries & Scorpio) and sits in eleventh house, it gives riches through great efforts and public dealings (political career), provides a dashing personality, but his mate may be quarrelsome and less cooperative which may lead him to go for another marriage. It is a great placement as regards benefits from property.*

Mars placed in the eleventh house if rules the 5ᵗʰ and the 12ᵗʰ houses (Aries & Scorpio), it may give mixed results. The native may have one son on whom he would need to spend a lot of money to bring him up and to giving him education. His spouse may be highly cultivated, communicative, caring and intelligent, and also a spendthrift. The native may have problems with friends and members of his family, as he may be curt in speech and in his dealings with them.

## Mercury Transiting the Eleventh House

When Mercury transits the eleventh house it provides a wide variety of friends mostly based on intellectual considerations. Such a native is often a social person, who is interested in communication and open-minded conversation, and exchanging information with others. Such a native is often dedicated to or inclined to the fields of science, astrology, intellectual pursuits, humanitarian causes and fields that require communicative abilities. The native is also inclined to writing work, publishing, printing, or in a business related to paper, cloth or food.

When Mercury owns the 1$^{st}$ and the 4$^{th}$ houses (Gemini & Virgo) and sits in the eleventh, it gives riches through business relating to the fields primarily communication; provides love and care from the mother, benefit from property, lives in good and comfortable houses, and has a good public image. When Mercury owns the 2$^{nd}$ and the 5$^{th}$ houses (Gemini & Virgo), it gives a couple of intelligent sons who support him financially in his old age; gives an artistic, caring and talented partner, and whose public image and support is great. When Mercury owns the 3$^{rd}$ and the 6$^{th}$ houses (Gemini & Virgo), it provides him great communicative ability. He is extremely good in speech and writing and likes teaching, editing and publishing for his vocation. He also likes to indulge in good partnership that gives him financial benefits.

*When Mercury owns 7$^{th}$ and the 10$^{th}$ houses (Gemini & Virgo) and sits in the eleventh house, it is a great placement as it provides him jobs relating to acting, dramatics, teaching and public-related fields connected more with women than men. He is highly respected by women and his mind is always busy helping the people to lift themselves financially and socially. He may have a partner who always supports him financially.*

When Mercury owns the 8th and the 11th houses (Gemini & Virgo) and sits in eleventh house, it is also a good placement as far as friendship with good and intellectual people is concerned. The native has a good public image, mostly chooses public-related jobs, and earns a lot of money through his own business. He may have some problems with his children as Mercury has debilitated aspects on the fifth house (Virgo in eleventh house). But when the sign Virgo rises in the 8th house, it provides good and intelligent children who are highly communicative too. When Mercury owns the 12th and 3rd houses (Gemini & Virgo) and sits in the eleventh house, it makes the person spend on his friends and brothers, his speech may be rude or curt at times. This placement may keep the individual often restless as he wants to do a lot but as he is inconsistent in his dealings and output, he is also less productive, which ultimately disturbs him.

## Jupiter Transiting the Eleventh House

Jupiter is connected with the native's success through groups of people and friends. It indicates growth through riches received through the stroke of luck and property, and money got from parents and ancestors. It also indicates success in large projects connected with humanitarian, religious, charitable and educational areas. It can also benefit the subject through travelling. The native is highly respected in his community when Jupiter is placed in the eleventh house of his chart.

*When Jupiter owns the 1st and the 4th houses (Sagittarius & Pisces) and sits in the eleventh house, it indicates great financial and property-related benefits through the parents. It provides at least one son who may excel in life, in status, and is later on nicely settled. The native is likely to be married at an early age comparatively and gets an intelligent and cooperative spouse.*

But Jupiter in the eleventh house in the sign Libra, which is its enemy's sign, may be productive of some kind of ill thoughts that may affect the conduct of the native by inducing anger or lack of ethical principles (as it owns the ascendant). When Jupiter owns the 2nd and the 5th houses (Sagittarius & Pisces) it indicates good financial status, and provides a couple of decent and highly placed sons. It may give a spouse who may be artistic in taste but less cooperative to the native having a different disposition. When Jupiter owns the 3rd and the 6th houses (Sagittarius & Pisces) and sits in the eleventh house, it helps the native to have good brothers, friends and a caring wife who is emotionally attached with him and brings luck to him. The native is very effortful but also creates enemies by his strict and highly disciplined disposition.

*When Jupiter owns the 4th and the 7th houses (Sagittarius & Pisces) and sits in the eleventh house, it is one of the best placements as it is in its exalted sign in the eleventh house. It provides a beautiful and educated spouse who is cooperative and supportive to the native. Jupiter in this placement is also indicative of good property and makes the native highly effortful and very effectively communicative. He may have a couple of sons who may be well placed but not always agreeing with the native.*

When Jupiter owns the 5th and the 8th houses (Sagittarius & Pisces) and sits in the eleventh, it gives a couple of intelligent sons, a pragmatic and devoted spouse and more number of sisters with whom his relationship may not be quite even. Socially, he is loved and highly respected by the people. He will be very agile and possess good life force to work. When Jupiter owns the 6th and the 9th houses (Sagittarius & Pisces), it indicates less success with the partners in business and provides a practical minded spouse who is quite attached to him and gives a couple of worthy children too. It provides him artistic talents and makes him effectively communicative.

*When Jupiter owns the 7th and the 10th houses (Sagittarius & Pisces), it is also a good placement as it gives the native riches and a very intelligent and religiously oriented spouse who is devoted to him. It indicates more number of daughters than sons and makes him socially respected by multitude of people. He is greatly effortful and liked by a good number of friends who are attached and devoted to him. When Jupiter owns the 8th and the 11th houses (Sagittarius & Pisces) it makes the native agile and spirited, full of energy, socially popular and highly accepted by his friends and the people he works with. He has a devoted but aggressive and moody kind of spouse. He may have a couple of influential brothers and friends who are always supportive to him.*

Jupiter sitting in the eleventh house and owning the 12th and the 3rd houses (Sagittarius & Pisces) indicates expenditure on friends and brothers. It gives him a highly cultured spouse who is very loving and caring. He may be highly communicative in speech and writing.

## Venus Transiting the Eleventh House

Venus indicates lots of friends and benefits from the association of people. It indicates idealism and financial growth for the subject. It is also connected with individual's social values and charitable causes. Venus inspires the native to possess artistic tastes, love for music and culture.

*When Venus owns the 1st and the 6th houses (Taurus & Libra) and sits in the eleventh house, it indicates great wealth earned through projects and partnership in business. The native will have leaning towards art and music and may take up acting and art-related jobs. His spouse may be aggressive and moody in disposition and he may have more daughters than sons. When Venus owns the ascendant (Taurus) and is in its exalted sign in the eleventh house, it provides the native an extremely charming personality, a great social status and support from the people and his community. It is by far one of the best placements of Venus in a chart except that he may have one daughter and no son.*

When Venus owns the 2nd and the 7th houses (Taurus & Libra) and sits in the eleventh house, it indicates great earnings and a very thoughtful, artistic and talented spouse who is devoted to the native. The native may have a son but quite late in life. When Venus owns the 3$^{rd}$ and the 8$^{th}$ houses (Taurus & Libra) and sits in the eleventh house, it gives more number of daughters, makes the person very effortful and communicative and provides him great physical strength and respect from the people. When Venus owns the 4$^{th}$ and the 9$^{th}$ houses (Taurus & Libra) and sits in the eleventh house, it gives the native great property but he has an accelerated lust to have more property and money. His relationship with the parents is uneven but he is lucky in earning money. He has quite a respectable social status too. When Venus owns 5$^{th}$ and 10$^{th}$ houses (Taurus & Libra) and sits in the eleventh house, it gives more number of daughters who are very intelligent and well placed in life. Such a native is well settled in life and benefited through government jobs. He is socially respected. When Venus owns 6$^{th}$ and 11$^{th}$ houses (Taurus & Libra) and sits in the eleventh, it gets the native great respect from the society. He is financially very rich and gets benefits from business partnerships. He has artistic talents and love for music. When Venus owns 7$^{th}$ and 12$^{th}$ houses (Taurus and Libra), it gives a spendthrift and intelligent spouse, he has less respect from his people and constantly keeps worrying to earn more and more. His travel plans are often less successful and bring more expenditure than the earnings.

*When Venus owns 11$^{th}$ and the 4$^{th}$ houses (Taurus & Libra), it is one of the best placements as it gives great job opportunity in the State revenue and finance departments, helps the native get support from the parents, he builds good houses and earns good money. He is also respected by his community and the people, and has a good social image too.*

## Saturn Transiting the Eleventh House

Saturn in the eleventh house indicates a few strong and meaningful friends. It does not accept any superficial sort of friendship. It indicates strong loyalty towards family, friends and people to whom he is closely attached. It deals with ideas, and ideas that lead to practical innovations. A well-placed Saturn in the eleventh house indicates strong organisational qualities, a good financial background and recognition from the people.

*When Saturn is placed in the eleventh house and owns the 1st and the 2nd houses, (Capricorn & Aquarius) it is quite an auspicious placement as regards the native's personal earnings are concerned. It makes him rich and affluent in life especially after 50 years of age. It makes him impulsive and secretive as well. The native is hard working, scientifically oriented, very practical in his outlook, has a lot of patience and is bestowed with a long life, more number of daughters and an emotionally rich spouse. The native may not be liked much by his co-workers as he is quite a strict disciplinarian. By far, it is one of the best placements of Saturn for it is very good job-wise and financially as well.*

When Saturn owns the 2nd and the 3rd houses (Capricorn & Aquarius), it makes a person quite communicative but still his conversation will be full of pragmatic kind of talks. He does not like extravagant discussions. As far as the native's finances are concerned, it is the best placement as it makes *Laxmi Yoga (Saturn rising in Libra in the eleventh house),* which means abundant money and prosperity. This *yoga* or placement is found in the charts of big businessman or industrialists. But the native, with such a placement, has less happiness from children or he may have hardly one child, a male possibly. He will be highly effortful, have good friends and prosperous brothers and quite a long life too. When Saturn owns the 4th and the 5th houses (Capricorn & Aquarius) and is placed in the eleventh house, it gives a couple of sons who will be well placed in life but may not have very smooth relationship with the native on account of his irritating and divergent conduct. But he will be highly influential, crafty and quite capable in planning and scheming things with which he will earn a great deal of money. When Saturn owns the 6th and 7th houses (Capricorn & Aquarius) and sits in the eleventh house, it makes the native very stiff in behaviour and eccentric kind of person in conduct as it aspects the ascendant which has

Leo rising. It is not a good aspect of Saturn and it may lead the native to cultivate some kind of ill habits, including drinking and gambling or involving in any other unsocial acts, which may give him less social support. This placement also helps him live long and may give him a spouse who is pragmatic but not much liked by the native as he is very ambitious and not practical.

When Saturn owns the 8$^{th}$ and the 9$^{th}$ houses (Capricorn & Aquarius) and sits in the eleventh house, it may help to provide him job/business relating to teaching, law and printing as well as books. It may also give a couple of sons who will be very intelligent and well settled in life. When Saturn owns the 10$^{th}$ and the 11$^{th}$ houses (Capricorn & Aquarius) and sits in the eleventh house, job-wise it is an excellent placement. It may provide jobs related to law, judiciary or administration, lucrative financially. The native may not have any children until quite late in life. It is also likely that the subject will be very crafty, be of a scheming nature, forming groups against his own friends and people with whom he works. He is an ambitious kind of person, as such he may have problems with his employer and friends as well. When Saturn owns 12$^{th}$ and the 1$^{st}$ houses and sits in the eleventh, it provides mixed results but makes a person quite affluent. At the same time, the native will need to spend a lot on family and friends.

### Rahu & Ketu Transiting the Eleventh House
Rahu & Ketu as well as any other planet rising in the eleventh house are always considered beneficial as far as one's finances are concerned.

**The aforesaid predictions are related to one planet only. The conjuncts with other planets are not explained with it as it would unnecessarily confuse the reader. However, if the reader goes through our first two books on astrology and gets the basic knowledge about the subject, it will not be difficult to comprehend what the conjuncts will bring to the native. Please keep in mind that** *placement, aspects and conjuncts of planets are very* *important factors* to form opinions about a house when considering predictions about it. Most of the placements relating to a house have been discussed by us in this book. Rest is left for the reader to decide, for everything cannot be put into small books.

## Analysis of the Charts

The following analysis of the charts (kundalis) will throw more light relating to the planets' positions, placements and aspects and enable the reader to comprehend more in that direction. We have tried to deduce certain precepts on the basis of various yogas, aspects and conjuncts formed in a chart in relation to the eleventh house and have presented them in bold and italics either at the beginning, middle or at the end when individual charts have been discussed.

## Case Study One

The following chart belongs to a retired Joint Director of Education in one of the western States in India. He was highly respected and identified as a good and honest administrator until he retired.

**Native born on 13ᵗʰ January, 1934**

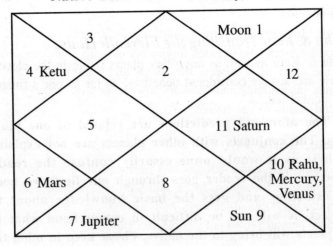

## Broad Analysis

When we analyse the chart given on the previous page and examine the position of the owner of the 11$^{th}$ house, we find that its owner, Jupiter, is placed in the 6$^{th}$ house in its enemy sign. Even then the native was highly respected by his colleagues when he was working in the education department at the State headquarters. He possessed a charming personality, conversed in a friendly manner and influenced people by his gentle demeanour. Probably two minus factors (the sixth house and Jupiter's transiting in the enemy sign) have given strength to Jupiter and benefited the native.

*The owner of the 11$^{th}$ Jupiter has aspects on the Moon and Saturn that own the 3$^{rd}$ house, and 9$^{th}$ & 10$^{th}$ houses respectively. As such he was always liked by women, had more number of sisters, and was respected by his senior officers for his gentle manners and honest disposition.*

As 11$^{th}$ house is related to riches and social status, the native was fairly rich and was respected by the people of his own community and by others as well. We cannot totally ignore the placement and position of the ascendant while examining the native's social status and gentle demeanour. Venus, the owner of ascendant, is placed in the 9$^{th}$ and is conjunct with Mercury which rules the 5$^{th}$ and the 2$^{nd}$ houses. It also provided him fair complexion, good personality and physique, and polite speech. Such characteristics are bound to confer status, respect and good finances too. Besides Jupiter being quite favourably placed in the chart as it aspects the Moon and Saturn, a well placed Venus (ascendant) and Mercury also helped in bestowing good social status to the native.

## Case Study Two

The following chart belongs to a businessman who hails from a rural area in Rajasthan, India, and who is a political leader too. Besides his political leanings, he is always considered a good and honest person on whom people can depend.

# Native born on 5<sup>th</sup> December, 1931

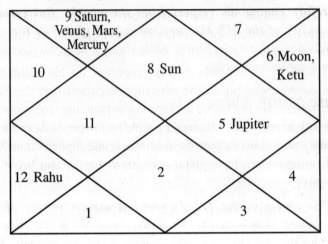

## Broad Analysis

*The owner of the 11<sup>th</sup> house, Mercury, is well conjunct with Mars, Venus and Saturn that own the ascendant, 7<sup>th</sup> and the 4<sup>th</sup> houses. The conjunct has taken place in the 2<sup>nd</sup> house which relates to hard earned money, family status and speech. The native is affluent in all these aspects in his life. It has certainly brought him great status in life. Currently, most politicians don't believe much in the traditional values but the native holds them very honestly. Consequently, he commands great respect from the people of his own community, and others too.*

Besides, the Sun, the owner of the 10<sup>th</sup>, is sitting in its friend's house at the ascendant. It has also boosted up the native's prestige and social status. It has already been stated that to earn a good reputation and social status it is the ascendant that also needs to be taken into account. In the above chart not only the ascendant is transiting in a friend's house (related with speech and fairly earned money), the Sun that owns the 10<sup>th</sup> house is also transiting the ascendant.

*A strong Sun always provides a good personality, energy, honest disposition, agility, straightforwardness, and many other manly qualities that can easily win other people's heart.*

*The native possess in abundance most of these qualities and therefore commands respect from the people. But certainly the owner of the 11th Mercury too is well placed in the chart which has helped him win a good social status, love from his own people and riches.*

## Case Study Three

The following chart belongs to a senior male nurse who has established a good status for himself by his hard work, knowledge and professional preparedness. He has been working in one of the government medical colleges in Rajasthan State in India.

**Native born on 12th September, 1954**

```
        5 Sun              3 Ketu
  6 Mercury    4 Jupiter           2
     7 Saturn,
      Venus             1
   8              10              12
     9 Mars,        11 Moon
      Rahu
```

### Broad Analysis

*When we examine the 11th house of the native's chart we find that its owner, Venus, is conjunct with an exalted Saturn in the 4th house. Besides, Venus rules the 2nd as well as the 4th house and is placed with its natural friend Saturn which is transiting in an exalted sign. Such a conjunct in itself is highly beneficial and may help in bringing riches, property, social status and support from parents as well.*

Unfortunately, Saturn's aspects on the 7th house are of debilitated nature, therefore, it has not permitted the native to attain a great status at his workplace (medical college, where he is simply a senior nurse), but in whatever position he is working in the government hospital, he is highly respected by the doctors and his senior colleagues. When a seriously indisposed person is brought to hospital and he is in care of the person, his opinion is also considered of great value by the doctors. At this point we need to examine other planets' position too to assess one's social status and riches. In the above chart, three planets—Jupiter, Mercury and Saturn—are exalted and two planets—the Sun and Venus—are transiting in their own signs. Their ownerships are also lucrative and financially helpful. In view of that it is so easy for the native to command great respect from the people of his own community and the people where he works.

## Case Study Four

The following chart belongs to a highly respected businessman who owns a lot of property, including a petrol pump in an affluent town in Rajasthan.

### Native born on 5th October, 1975

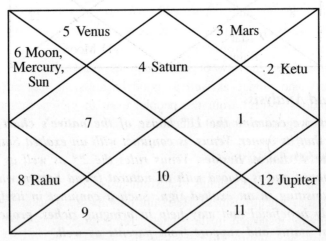

## Broad Analysis

*Venus as the ruler of the 11th and 4th houses is rising in the 2nd house which is the house of personal earnings or gains through right efforts. It forms a kind of Laxmi Yoga, which brings riches and property to the native.* Throughout the world when people own a lot of property, land and money, they are respected in the society even if they don't share their money or property with others. But if the native is a philanthropist, the amount of respect he wins is phenomenal. The native whose chart we are examining has three benefic planets placed in the 3rd house. Mercury is exalted in the 3rd and is conjunct with the ascendant Moon and a strong Sun that rules the 2nd house in the chart. Such placements and conjuncts provide the native a kind and highly friendly and emotional temperament, attached to his brothers, sisters and friends, and always ready to help them. It also makes him lucky as all these three planets aspect the 9th house and in return Jupiter also aspects them from the ninth.

Again, a strong Ketu rising in a friendly sign also benefits the native. It provides him a kind of sixth sense required to be a good and clever businessman. The native has a petrol station at a conspicuous place in Rajasthan. It gives him regular income and adds to his status and social prestige. Saturn, ruler of the 7th and the 8th houses is transiting the ascendant of the chart. It provides him a steady temperament, pragmatic character and farsightedness. In view of such qualities, possessing a lot of property and money as well as good business, he has earned tremendous respect from the people, even though he has not been very good in formal education.

# Case Study Five

The following chart belongs to a Mumbai-based person engaged in pharmaceutical business. He is not only extremely rich, he is also highly respected in the society. Temperamentally, he does not show any agility. He talks less and means more.

# Native born on 17<sup>th</sup> November, 1969

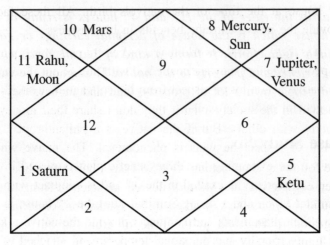

## Broad Analysis

*When we examine the 11<sup>th</sup> house in the chart of the native, we find Jupiter and Venus conjunct at the 11<sup>th</sup> house. Jupiter being the owner of the ascendant and Venus as the ruler of 11<sup>th</sup> are very important planets rising in the 11<sup>th</sup> house in a chart. It predicts great riches and profits by fair or odd means. It also shows a kind of restless and a less productive disposition as both the planets are natural enemies and are conjunct in a very important house—the house of benefits and riches. But Saturn has aspects on both the planets making the native very clever, determined, desirous to win the race and affecting the native's thinking in different ways which provides him ideas to expand his business and earn more. Please note that Saturn being the owner of the 2<sup>nd</sup> and 3<sup>rd</sup>, when aspects the ascendant in the 11<sup>th</sup> house provides not only riches, clever determination and a desire to expand, it also makes the native work hard and be productive.* Therefore, it also cancels the odd aspects (to some extent) that result because Jupiter as an ascendant is conjunct with Venus. There is also a kind of **Laxmi Yoga** in the chart that makes him extremely rich. The owners of the 2<sup>nd</sup> Saturn and 11<sup>th</sup> Venus being natural friends have mutual aspects. Besides, an exalted Mars transits in the 2nd house at the time of the native's birth. All these factors provide the native extreme benefits in his business.

It is the way of the world that a successful person is honoured by people whether they are connected with him or not. Therefore, the native gets a lot of respect from his colleagues, workers and the general public as well.

## Case Study Six

The following chart belongs to a Sri Lanka-born gentleman who, after completing his Masters degree in science from Madras around 40 years back, worked in Sri Lanka for some time. He migrated to England at the time of ethnic disturbances in Sri Lanka. He worked in West Africa for almost 14 years as head of the science department before finally going back to England. Right now (2007) he is residing in London.

**Native born on 29th May, 1938**

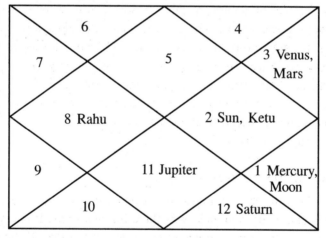

### *Broad Analysis*

When we examine the chart of the native, we observe that *both Mars and Venus—the rulers of the 9th and the 10th houses—are conjunct at the 11th house auspiciously forming a kind of strong Rajyoga. It provides the native not only regular good positions in government-owned institutions or established institutions, but also helps him earn a lot of money through his jobs.* The 11$^{th}$ house also has aspects from a strong Jupiter which is the owner of the 5$^{th}$ house related to education. As such, the native always got great opportunities to work in educational institutions. After 14 years of good and productive work in West Africa, when he came back to England, he easily got a lucrative teaching job in an institution in London. Although the owner of the ascendant has aspects from Saturn that affected the native's productivity, his lifestyle and also thinking process adversely to some extent, but good aspects on the ascendant by Jupiter restored good thinking and provided him a hard working demeanour which made him fairly productive in his plans and projects. Mercury is also conjunct with a strong Moon and well placed in the chart. It rules the 11$^{th}$ house and has aspects on the 3$^{rd}$ house. The 3$^{rd}$ also has aspects from a benefic Jupiter. As such, the native's working capability was doubled and the ill effects of Saturn on the ascendant, Sun, were lessened. He was observed to be working very hard and always planning ahead for his future projects. As his 11$^{th}$ and the ascendant possess good aspects and the 11$^{th}$ is enriched by *yogakarak* conjuncts (Mars and Venus), the native commanded a lot of respect from his countrymen in Africa and is well known and respected by his friends and compatriots in England, too, besides possessing great riches.

## Case Study Seven

The following chart belongs to a London-based Indian banker who is extremely rich and owns three big mansions. It is a very strong case of a native in whose chart the 3$^{rd}$ and the 11$^{th}$ houses are very strong from the nativity on account of good placement and aspects of the planets.

# Native born on 28th April, 1980

```
┌─────────────────────────────────────────┐
│  5 Mars,        4    │    2 Venus         │
│  Saturn,             │                    │
│  Jupiter,         3  │         1 Sun      │
│  Rahu                │                    │
│      6 Moon          │    12 Mercury      │
│   7          9       │         11 Ketu    │
│          8       │       10               │
└─────────────────────────────────────────┘
```

## Broad Analysis

*If we observe the chart carefully, we find an exalted Sun rising in the 11<sup>th</sup> house which provides the native riches and honours from his people. Besides, there is an exchange of the owners of the 3<sup>rd</sup> and the 11<sup>th</sup> houses—Sun and Mars, which provides the native riches, fortitude, hard working disposition, respect from his own community and other people, and also makes him very effortful. Besides, a strong Jupiter aspects the Sun and is conjunct with Mars and the owner of the 9<sup>th</sup>, Saturn. It has provided the native farsightedness, good relationship with friends, except that Rahu's placement in the sign Leo would create some problems with a few friends, brothers or relatives. It also makes the native highly effortful except that some of his efforts may not yield fruitful results as Rahu may bring some adverse results too.*

It has already been related that to measure one's riches, status and honours, it is also worthwhile to examine the position of the ascendant. In the above case, the ascendant Mercury is placed in the 10<sup>th</sup> house from its ownership. Although Mercury is in its debilitated sign, it has formed **Neechbhanga Yoga.** That means it is cancelling itself its rising in the debilitation sign as it is placed in the 10<sup>th</sup> house from its own house ascendant. Thus, Mercury becomes highly *yogakarak*. Besides, the owner of the ascendant, Mercury, is also the ruler of the 4<sup>th</sup> house. Thus, it has become very strong and fruitful. Not only as an ascendant but also as the owner of the 4<sup>th</sup> house, it has constantly provided the native good results. Consequently, he has been getting a lot of recognition from his own community in London. English people also recognise him as a good person. Mercury, as the owner of the 4<sup>th</sup> and having aspects on it, has bestowed on the native benefits of property. It is because of this that he owns a number of great mansions in London. His staying in a foreign land is caused on account of Saturn, which as the owner of the 9<sup>th</sup> also has aspects on the 9<sup>th</sup>. * Therefore, one must keep in view other factors too in a chart before predicting about a certain house or a certain issue. *The 11<sup>th</sup> house and the placement of its owner are very important factors to predict one's riches and social status, but it is equally important that ascendant, the 4<sup>th</sup> and the 9<sup>th</sup> houses and the owners of these houses should also be taken into consideration while predictions are made about one's riches, status and property.*

## Case Study Eight

The following chart belongs to a senior lecturer working in an established college affiliated to a reputed University in the northern part of India. She is very smart, extremely fluent, highly communicative in conversation, and is endowed with an exemplary demeanour.

---

\* To find out details about the 9<sup>th</sup> house from our book, **Explore The Power of Astrology: Trikona One,** published by Unicorn Books (2006)

## Native born on 7th September, 1955

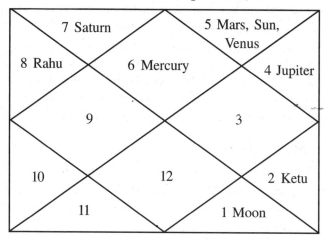

## Broad Analysis

It is another good example of a native in whose chart an exalted Jupiter is placed the 11th house and has made great contribution to her personal reputation although she became widow at an early age when her daughter was still small. Jupiter has aspects on the 3rd, 5th and the 7th houses too. That has provided her good education, property and initially a caring husband too.

*Three planets in the chart are exalted: Jupiter, Mercury and Saturn. The Sun in Leo is transiting in its own house. All these have contributed to her possessing a good and comely bearing, efficient conversational power, a carefree nature having an attitude to help others and to spend as much as she likes, riches and property as well.*

The Sun in Leo has also bestowed on her great strength of character, reputation, status and great liking for her by her colleagues. Most of the senior staff knows her well and recognises her as a good person. She is well informed because the owner of the ascendant, Mercury, is sitting in its exalted sign at the *lagna*. It also makes her highly communicative and bestows agility.

As we are limiting our discussion in this section only to the 11th house and matters related to it, we are not going far about other details relating to her marriage. But if we observe carefully we find that in spite of good aspects from Jupiter on the 7th house, both Mars and Mercury have malefic aspects on the 7th house of the native. Consequently, her husband died a few years after her marriage. But her 11th house and the ascendant, too, certainly add to her status, finances, and social prestige.

## Case Study Nine

The following chart belongs to a lady eye doctor who is recognised by her relatives, friends and patients. She is a well organised housewife, a good human being, and possesses a compassionate nature as a doctor.

### Native born on 28th July, 1963

## *Broad Analysis*

When we examine the native's chart carefully, we find several good aspects on beneficial planets like Jupiter, Mars, Sun and Mercury and also on their houses. For example, the owners of the 11th and 10th houses have mutual aspects on each other. It provides her good financial benefit from her job and indicates huge gain of property from her husband and parents as well. As Jupiter has aspects on the 2nd and the 4th houses, it indicates lots of property gains. Jupiter has aspects on Mercury, the owner of the ascendant, which is rising in the 2nd house. It fortifies her against any health hazards, protects her against any odd conditions that arise as a result of Saturn's aspects on the Sun sitting in the 2nd house. Jupiter also has aspects on the Sun which provides the native benefits from her brother and friends.

*Thus, a well placed Mars which is the owner of the 11th and a strong Jupiter rising in its own sign in the 10th house, with their mutual aspects on each other, have greatly benefited the native. It has not only bestowed upon her property and financial gains, but has also earned her good reputation as a doctor and a human being. Mercury and the Sun's conjunct has also added to her imaginative and calculative capability as well as helping her in adding to the family income.*

## Case Study Ten

The following chart belongs to an MBA student who is likely to pass out after one and a half years from the time (2007) this chart is being analysed. He is a fairly young person, who possesses an attractive personality and is well known by his colleagues and friends. He is a decent human being.

### Native born on 3rd December, 1982

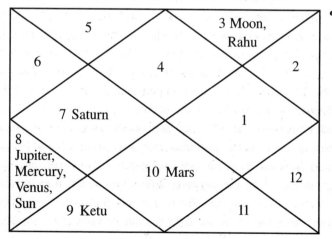

## Broad Analysis

Like some other charts which we have discussed in this section of the book, *this chart also projects a good 11<sup>th</sup> house which is strong and which has aspects from four important planets that rule the 9<sup>th</sup>, 10<sup>th</sup>, 11<sup>th</sup>, 2<sup>nd</sup>, and 3<sup>rd</sup> houses. Venus, which is the owner of the 4<sup>th</sup> and the 11<sup>th</sup> houses, rises in the 5<sup>th</sup> house and aspects the 11<sup>th</sup> house. Likewise Jupiter, Sun and Mercury also have their aspects on the 11<sup>th</sup> house. All these planets' aspects determine or indicate good financial status of the native after 27 years. A kind of Laxmi Yoga is also present in the chart as the owners of the 2<sup>nd</sup> and the 11<sup>th</sup> are conjunct in the 5<sup>th</sup> house and have their direct aspects on the 11<sup>th</sup> house. It indicates not only riches and property, but an extraordinary memory, great logical capability, goal-oriented attitude, research-mindedness, and great communicative ability, except that Venus and Jupiter being conjunct in the 5<sup>th</sup> house reduces the aforesaid gains to some extent.*

Two planets—Saturn and Mars—exalt in the chart and have their aspect on the 10<sup>th</sup> house. Consequently, the native will always be getting job opportunities but will also be changing jobs as Saturn has debilitated aspects on the 10<sup>th</sup> house. Jupiter as the owner of 9<sup>th</sup>, aspects the 9<sup>th</sup> house too. It provides opportunities for higher education and to work and visit foreign countries. Jupiter has exalted aspects on the ascendant. It provides great strength of character to the native. The Moon is conjunct with Rahu in the 12<sup>th</sup> house at the nativity. Moon's unfruitful transit in the 12<sup>th</sup> house has been compensated by the benefic aspects of Jupiter. Thus, in totality, the native is likely to be benefited by good aspects on the 10<sup>th</sup>, 11<sup>th</sup> and on the ascendant. An exalted Saturn in the 4<sup>th</sup> house also indicates foreign travels and property-related benefits from mother and parents. However, an exalted Mars in the 7<sup>th</sup> house suggests difficulties in the married life of the native. Yet, aspects from a good number of *yogakarak* planets from the 5<sup>th</sup> house help the native earn great wealth and

social status. It also gives him opportunity to be socially well
known and popular with his mates and co-workers.

## Case Study Eleven

The native was born in an affluent family in Uttar Pradesh and
was reared up by wealthy parents with great care and affection
as she was the only daughter in their family. When she was
young she fell in love with an Indian who had migrated to the
US. The parents gave her away in marriage as she had desired.
Unfortunately, she returned home after leaving her husband's
home in about two years and joined her parents in their business
for she thought she could not continue with her man any more.

**Native born on 20th April, 1962**

| | | |
|---|---|---|
| 2 | 1 Sun, Venus, Mercury | 12 Mars |
| 3 | | 11 Jupiter |
| 4 Rahu | | 10 Saturn, Ketu |
| 5 | 7 Moon | 9 |
| 6 | | 8 |

*Broad Analysis*

When we examine the above chart we find some unusual
conjuncts and aspects that have affected the native's personality
in various ways. The owner of the 11th Saturn is rising in the
10th house conjunct with Ketu. Jupiter, the owner of the 9th, is
rising in the 11th house. Both Jupiter and Saturn have their aspects
on the Moon. As such it has provided the native a mixed
temperament. She is easily elated and soon gets annoyed on

matters not much concerning her. But an exalted Sun, ruler of the 5<sup>th</sup>, has also provided her an intelligent personality, with an ability to take quick decisions and be good in handling projects of business or academic nature. Venus and Mercury are also conjunct with the exalted Sun at the ascendant. That has added much charm to her personality. Not only is she highly fascinating, she has artistic tastes too. It is quite unfortunate that besides a benefic Jupiter's aspects on the 7<sup>th</sup> house, Saturn, Mars and Sun also aspect that house jeopardising matters relating to the 7<sup>th</sup> house. If we examine the chart further, we observe that Venus and Mercury also aspect the 7<sup>th</sup> house. It certainly has affected the 7<sup>th</sup> house of the native. She appears highly attractive to men but she is not able to take decisions in her favour. Besides, she is also actively cooperating with her father and brother in their business.

In view of the above discussions, the native has obviously been getting great ovation from the people she meets, especially the business partners, and the clients related to property and business.

*Therefore, a strong 11<sup>th</sup> house (as Jupiter is transiting in that house) and a strong ascendant where three important planets are conjunct, are likely to provide her honour and respect from the people she meets. It also helps her to be rich independently.*

## Case Study Twelve

The following chart belongs to a young man of great talents and attractive personality who in his early age has reached quite a high position and status. Currently he is the Manager of Hutch Telecom Company in a big town in Rajasthan. He is dashing, intelligent, agile, a spendthrift, good-looking and possesses a decent demeanour with which he easily wins people and clients.

## Native born on 2nd July, 1979

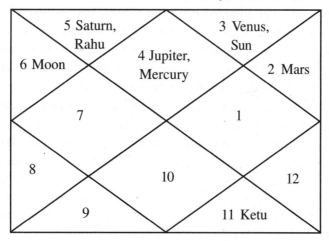

## Broad Analysis

When we carefully examine the native's chart, we find the owner of the 11th, Venus, and the owner of the 2nd, Sun, conjunct in the 12th house which is considered as the house of waste, expenditure and travelling. In view of that, the native's reputation could be at stake and this conjunct is also going to affect his finances on account of his spendthrift nature caused by the planets that own the 2nd, 3rd and 11th houses. *But there are other aspects on the 11th house and the owner of the 5th and the 10th houses as well that have decreased the ill effects of Venus-Sun conjunct in the 12th. It is Saturn's aspects on Mars sitting in the 11th house. It has turned the scales in his favour. Saturn as the owner of 7th and 8th aspects the owner of the 10th, Mars, which is the owner of the 5th too. It provides the native opportunity to study and work in technical fields.* Besides, Mars as the owner of the 5th house also aspects the 5th house. Thus, Saturn's aspects on Mars and Mars' aspects on its own sign rising in the 5th house helps the native to acquire education in scientific and technological fields.

There are some other important factors that need the reader's attention. These are: the ascendant Moon sitting in the 3rd has its benefic aspects on the 9$^{th}$ house ruled by Jupiter, its permanent friend. It provides the native benefit from foreign travels and helps in attaining higher education in foreign lands. Besides, the owner of the 9$^{th}$, Jupiter, sitting in an exalted position at the ascendant also has aspects on the 9$^{th}$ house. It further confirms attainment of higher education and foreign travels.

Thus, the ill effects of the owner of the 11$^{th}$ house transiting in the 12$^{th}$ house may not be completely experienced as bad by the native. Besides, Venus rising in the 12$^{th}$ is often considered less malefic. Tradition says Venus in the 12$^{th}$ rising in a friend's sign or in a benefic sign often provides good results. It appears that the native's strong ascendant and the benefic Mars are going to redeem him from so many ill effects caused on account of the company of women and expensive friends.

## Case Study Thirteen

The following chart belongs to a very famous American actress, Katharine Hepburn, born in Connecticut, USA at 5.47 P.M. in the fifth month when the Sun was exalted in the horizon. She became famous as her career advanced in the cinema world and was gradually considered one of the most famous and celebrated people in Hollywood.

### Native born on 12$^{th}$ May, 1907

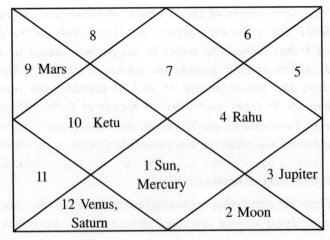

## Broad Analysis

The owner of the 11$^{th}$, Sun, is exalted and conjunct with the owner of the 9$^{th}$, Mercury, in the 7$^{th}$ house which is also related to profession. It indicates great support from a highly placed spouse who was instrumental in bringing her good luck and position. The chart is endowed with three exalted planets—Venus, Moon and Sun. Exalted Venus which rules the ascendant and the 8$^{th}$ houses, is conjunct with Saturn in the 6$^{th}$ house which is a benefic house for Saturn and Venus too. The exalted Sun in the 7$^{th}$ may not be as good for the mate, but it is conjunct with the owner of the 9$^{th}$, therefore it has become quite auspicious. Mars has aspects on the exalted Venus, the owner of the ascendant. It bestowed on her stage and cinema-related talents. Besides, Sun and Mercury's aspects on the ascendant conferred upon her the art of speech and communication abilities required for a stage or cinema person. The owner of the 10$^{th}$ Moon is exalted and transits in the 11$^{th}$ house from its ownership. The 8$^{th}$ house is instrumental in bestowing strength and great zeal to a native. She possessed that kind of demeanour and was distinctly eloquent in her speech. Although any planet in the 10$^{th}$ house becomes *yogakarak* but Rahu placed in its enemy sign adversely affected her career in the beginning. But soon the exalted Sun, Venus and Moon took over and provided her the talents and opportunities that mounted her to the highest ladder in the Western cinema world.

*We have already expressed that besides the 11$^{th}$ house and its owner, one should also take into consideration the position and the placement of the ascendant if status, social prestige and riches are to be reckoned. In this respect, the above chart clearly endorses the precepts drawn from the analysis of the charts given in this section of the book.*

## Case Study Fourteen

The following chart belongs to another famous actor of Hollywood who suddenly became renowned during the early fifties in the

20th century when his movie "On The Waterfront" got recognition in the Western world. By the time his other movie "The Godfather" was released, he was already nominated for the award of the best actor. Marlon Brando was born at Omaha in Nebraska, USA.

## Native born on 3rd April, 1924

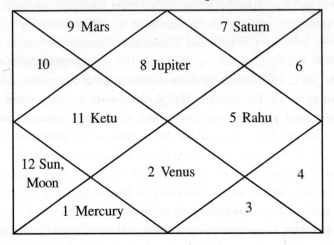

## Broad Analysis

Although the owner of the 11th Mercury is rising in the 6th house but astrologically sixth house belongs to Mercury. As such its placement in the 6th is good, more so because it also owns the 8th house. That way it forms *Vipreet Rajyoga* which brings him riches and affluence. There is an extremely good exchange of *yogakarak* planets in the chart that inspired him to work in the field of cinema. The owner of the ascendant, Mars, and the owner of the 5th house, Jupiter, have exchanged their houses. It not only provided him acting talents (Mars) but also riches and sharp insight that helped him to understand and play correctly the roles he was given. A strong Jupiter transiting at the ascendant aspects both, the Moon and the Sun that own the 9th and the 10th houses respectively. Thus, the owners of the 9th, 10th and the 5th are in conjunction on account of Jupiter's aspects on them. It forms a strong **Rajyoga** that generally bestows honours, riches and great status. Marlon Brando did possess all that and was highly respected in the Western cinema world. Let us not undermine the aspects of an exalted Saturn on the ascendant Mars, making him secretive and practical in his life. Besides, Venus rising in its own sign at the 7$^{th}$ house also aspects the ascendant and Jupiter. Although mutual exchange of aspects of Jupiter and Venus may not be taken as very lucrative, it did provide him a critical insight required to play correct roles in different situations.

*In fact, in Marlon Brando's case it is the exchange of the owners of 1$^{st}$ and the 5$^{th}$ houses and aspects from a benefic Jupiter on the owners of the 9$^{th}$ and 10$^{th}$ houses that have brought him much in life than only by the owner of the 11$^{th.}$ It provides us an idea that exchanges between two friendly planets and aspects from the benefic and friendly planets on the planets that are considered natural friends, may always be highly fruitful, productive and may provide riches, status, fame and social prestige to any native in whose chart such yogas appear. In that respect Marlon Brando was extremely lucky.*

## The Concluding Chart

Before concluding this chapter we like to present before the reader one more chart to indicate that if the owner of the 11$^{th}$ house is well placed in a chart, it may cover up so many inadequacies relating to ill aspects or weak placements of the planets that affect the native's life and career adversely. Let us present it before the reader with a concrete example.

In fact, we have already discussed and analysed initially the following chart in our first book on astrology—**Explore the Power of Astrology.** The chart belongs to a well placed and highly progressive Electronic Engineer based in USA. He was born (4.22 AM) on 3$^{rd}$ March in 1962 in India. After graduating in Electronic Engineering from USA, he took up a job in the US around 1988. Since then he is on the road to progress. He has developed some kind of expertise in the field of verification of chips that has brought him great success in his field and helped him to get an annual salary more than $180000.

**Native born on 3rd March, 1962**

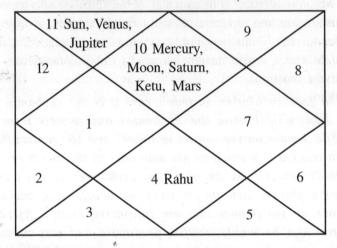

## Specific Discussions

All planets are never placed in good and benefic houses in a chart. The native's chart also does not reflect that every *yogakarak* planet is well placed in the chart. There are a couple of planets that are not well placed and reflect their ill effects. For example, Jupiter as the ruler of 12th and 3rd conjunct with Venus and placed in the 2nd house is not quite a favourable placement as far as the native's earnings are concerned. Although a benefic Venus is rising in the 2nd house (5th from 10th and 10th from 2nd), but it being conjunct with Jupiter has caused changing various jobs and financial losses. In this respect some of his decisions were good but some not quite acceptable as far as his progress is concerned. It has happened mainly on account of Venus-Jupiter conjunct in the 2nd house dragging the native into two different directions. The Sun, as the owner of the 8th, is also conjunct with Jupiter and Venus in the 2nd house, but it does not add any strength to Venus which is *yogakarak* in the chart being the ruler of the 5$^{th}$ and the 10$^{th}$ houses, except that it provides him strength in speech and good family background. Rahu's placement in the 7$^{th}$ house rising in its enemy's sign has distorted the matters relating to the 7$^{th}$ house. The owner of the 7$^{th}$ Moon is conjunct with Saturn at the ascendant which provides constant anxiety and concern from the mate and also various other kinds of apprehensions. But Moon's conjunct with Mars and Mercury, its permanent friends, is good and provides the native an optimistic attitude, good flight of imagination, capacity to think critically, scientist's insight, and a hope bearing demeanour.

*Well, all the above findings are somehow related to the 11$^{th}$ house or its owner as the Moon and Mercury are conjunct with Mars. It indicates a good emotional conduct and reveals a thoughtful intelligent outlook towards life. In fact, one of the best placements in the chart is an exalted Mars (the owner of the 11$^{th}$ and 4$^{th}$) conjunct with a strong Saturn, owner of the ascendant. It forms benefic yogas to make the native a great engineer who will earn a great deal of money, prestige, social status and fame in his future.*

*Although Jupiter, the owner of the 12$^{th}$ (house of waste, expenditure & travel) and the 3$^{rd}$ (house of efforts & friends etc.) is transiting the 2$^{nd}$ house which is the house of hard earned money and which is instrumental to spend a lot on his family (2$^{nd}$ house is related to family & speech, etc) and may foil his progressive plans, but an exalted Mars conjunct with Saturn, the owner of the 2$^{nd}$ and the ascendant has mitigated much of the ill effects of Jupiter. Besides, the conjunct of the owner of the 2$^{nd}$, Saturn, and the owner of the 11$^{th}$, Mars, forms a kind of Laxmi Yoga (bestows riches), which mitigates ill effects relating to the native's earnings and savings. A strong ascendant, Saturn, has aspects on the 3$^{rd}$ house. It helps the native to possess scientific temper, to be practical, doggedly effortful and to reach the desired goals. But he may experience sometimes ill effects too caused* *by Jupiter-Venus conjunct, primarily being indecisive when important matters need to be decided positively.*

## Brief Summary of Results

*The reader must keep in view the placements of the ascendant, the owners of the 4th, the 5th and the 10th houses when analysing and predicting matters relating to the 11th house. In fact, primarily it is the ascendant and the owner of the 11th that bestow riches, good nature, choice of profession, success, social status and affluence of every kind to a native, besides the owners of the 10th and the 9th houses.*

*When the owners of the 11th and the 1st houses are conjunct with each other in a benefic house like ascendant, 4th, 5th, 9th, 10th, or 11th house, they become highly beneficial or yogakarak, and bestow upon the native affluence relating to money, property, social status, sudden gains and peace of mind. Such conjuncts or mutual aspects make the native highly effortful providing happiness, enrichment of various kinds, benefits and love from his own people and parents. This concludes our discussion relating to the 11th house.*

# Bibliography

**Trikona** *Two*

1. Campbell, Elizabeth Rose (2003) Intuitive Astrology; New York: Ballantine Books.

2. Cox, Kathleen; (2000); Vastu Living; New York: Marlowe & Company Publication.

3. Editors—Time-Life Books(1990)Mysteries of the Unknown: Cosmic Connections; Virginia: Time-Life Books.

4. Gerwick-Brodeur, Madeline and Lenard, Lisa; (2003); The Complete Idiot's Guide To Astrology; (2003); New York: Alpha Books.

5. Goldschneider, Gary (1994), The Secret Language of Birthdays; Middlesex, England: Penguin Books.

6. Huntley, Janis; (1998); Astrology; London: Element Books.

7. Lewis, James R., (1994) The Astrology Encyclopaedia, Detroit, Washington D.C.: Gale Research Inc.

8. Parashar A. P. & V. K.; (2005), Explore the Power of Astrology; New Delhi: Unicorn Books.

9. Parashar A.P. & V.K.; (2006) Explore the Power of Astrology: Trikona One; New Delhi: Unicorn Books.

10. Parker, Julia & Derek (2000); Guide To Astrology; London: Dorling Kindersley Publication.

11. Parker, Julia & Derek (1991) Parkers' Astrology: New Edition; London: A DK Publishing Book.

12. Snodgrass, Mary Ellen (1997) Signs of The Zodiac; London: Greenwood Press.

13. Tester, Jim, (1987) A History of Western Astrology; New York: Ballantine Books.

14. The American AstroAnalysis Institute, (1976) AstroAnalysis: The Capricorn Personality; New York: Berkley Books.

15. The Everything Astrology Book, (2006); Massachusetts, Avon: Adams Media.

16. White, Suzanne, (1986), The New Astrology; New York: St. Martin's Press.

17. William W. Hewitt, (1991) Astrology for Beginners; St Paul, Minnesota: Lewellyn Publications.

18. Woolfolk, Joanna Martine; (2001) The Only Astrology Book You'll Ever Need: Madison Books: New York; Lanham.

# Appendices

# The Zodiac Signs

Since ancient times astrologers in India always recognised 12 zodiac signs. During the past few centuries astrologers in the West have also recognised 12 familiar zodiac signs through which all the planets march past. We now look at how the zodiac signs are identified and associated with certain major personal characteristics. Long time ago, the star constellations that lie behind 30-degree segments of the zodiac were given the names they now have because the star patterns were thought to look like those figures. 'Through the centuries, however, and because of irregularity in the Earth's revolution on its axis as it revolves around the Sun, the sky that the ancients observed has "shifted." In fact, the fixed stars (constellations) that the zodiac signs are named after have moved slowly backwards in the sky. It has a process called the "precession of the equinoxes." *

However, the names, the dates and the zodiac signs the Sun transits every month are given in the following table for the immediate reference of the reader.

---

\* The stars have moved so much that the zodiac signs are no longer in their original constellation. (10: p. 54)

## TABLE 1: Names, dates and the figures of the zodiac signs

| | | | |
|---|---|---|---|
| Aries | 14<sup>th</sup> April to 13<sup>th</sup> May | | (Ram) |
| Taurus | 14<sup>th</sup> May to 13<sup>th</sup> June | | (Bull) |
| Gemini | 14<sup>th</sup> June to 13-14 July | | (Twins) |
| Cancer | 14<sup>th</sup> July to 13-14 August | | (Crab) |
| Leo | 14<sup>th</sup> August to 13-14 Sept. | | (Lion) |
| Virgo | 15<sup>th</sup> Sept. to 13<sup>th</sup> October | | (Virgin) |
| Libra | 14<sup>th</sup> Oct. to 13<sup>th</sup> November | | (Scales) |
| Scorpio | 14<sup>th</sup> Nov. to 13-14 Dec. | | (Scorpio) |
| Sagittarius | 14<sup>th</sup> Dec. to 13<sup>th</sup> January | | (Archer) |
| Capricorn | 14<sup>th</sup> Jan. to 13<sup>th</sup> February | | (Goat) |
| Aquarius | 14<sup>th</sup> Feb. to 13<sup>th</sup> March | | (Water Bearer) |
| Pisces | 14<sup>th</sup> March to 13<sup>th</sup> April | | (Two Fish) |

**ARIES** *(Mesha)*
April 14—May 13

# Main Attributes

Aries, being the first sign of the zodiac, symbolises new beginnings. Certainly one can say that an Aries' life is adventurous. There is a dynamic restlessness in Aries' life. One born with the Sun in Aries becomes an activist and a doer. Outwardly an Aries appears to be talkative, vibrant and exciting. Most Aries people are direct, outspoken and uncomplicated. Such natives are greatly exciting and demonstrative. They are generous to a fault and at times highly affectionate. An Aries is a natural leader and possesses great confidence. The native is generous, a natural-born warrior, and courageous. An Aries is warm and ardent in human relationships. There is nothing half-hearted. In fact, independence is the key word of his nature. He is willing to gamble his plans, follow a dream, set the mind on a goal and pursue it with great enthusiasm. Optimism is his supreme quality, but sometimes such an individual lacks tact and diplomacy. (18: p. 9-10)

An Aries person can become a good executive, police officer, fire fighter, film stunt person, ambulance driver, film director, soldier, sales representative, iron or steel worker, an athlete, a racing car driver and a circus performer. (6: p. 14) An Aries is energetic, assertive, urgent, strong-minded, quick, planned, straightforward, enthusiastic, selfish, possesses initiative, impulsive, fiery, mostly positive and outgoing in nature, and adventurous. He possesses a sense of self-respect, high energy levels, is highly competitive, loves taking risks, hot-headed and rude. Regardless of obstacles he possess an energetic determination to fulfil his work. (10: p. 55)

**TAURUS (*Vrishabha*)**

May 14—June 13

# Main Attributes

A native born with the sign Taurus often survives when others fall by the wayside. As perseverance is a characteristic required for success, the Taurus person tends to be  successful. His strength resides in firmness and steady drive. He is a purposeful achiever and possesses endless patience to see a thing through. A Taurus individual is patient but when he is opposed he becomes angry. Unless someone seriously provokes him, he is gentle. A Taurus person is quiet and gentle but he knows his own mind and therefore, nothing can dissuade him when once convinced. This sign possesses a lot of firmness and usually is strong enough, physically and mentally, to overcome most of life's obstacles. Such a person is caring. He is affectionate and possesses a great liking for all beautiful things. He/she is bestowed with genuine creative gifts and is highly inspired by art and music.

A Taurus individual can be a farmer, construction worker, forest ranger, domestic worker, cook, stockbroker, accountant, financial adviser, architect, work in theatres, painter, hotelier, bank manager, musician, singer, teacher, dress designer. (6: p. 18) A Taurus person is often possessive, reliable, loyal, stubborn and lazy. He is persistent, romantic, charming, affectionate, warm, beautiful, self-indulgent, lover of luxury and comfort.

**GEMINI (*Mithuna*)**

June 14—July 13-14

# Main Attributes

The native born with the sign Gemini is many-sided, quick in thought and action, clever with words, quite skilful at handling others and full of new ideas. Most astrologers consider Gemini as a human sign because it possesses qualities that are akin to humans, such as intelligence, adaptability, and communicativeness.

People born in Gemini sign do good in professions like teaching, law and politics. They love to be as actors, journalists, dancers and entertainers. Such people also love modelling, acrobats and oratory. They are very happy in jobs like airport workers and travel consultants. (6: p. 22) They enjoy writing and chatting with people. A Gemini individual is highly perceptive and can quickly pick up information here and gossip there. This makes him an ideal conversationalist. He has a gift of writing, speaking and self-expression. A Gemini can adapt to many kinds of situations and deal with different sorts of people. As a Gemini individual is highly amusing, versatile and witty, he can lift people out of their problems.

In fact, Gemini people need mental challenges to keep them busy on the job and it cannot be the same challenge over and over again. They love careers like advertising, writing, broadcasting, and public relations. Such a native possesses an inquiring mind and is a good salesperson too. Briefly, a Gemini is versatile, communicative, witty, intellectual, sharp, restless, lively, quick-witted, detests boredom, and possesses ability to do several things at a time. (12: p. 57)

### CANCER (Kerka)
July 14—August 13-14

## Main Attributes

A native born with Cancer sign may be gentle, kind and sympathetic. A person with Cancer sign may often be complex, fragile, unpredictable, temperamental, and may need constant support and encouragement. Such a native wants desperately to be loved and approved of. His greatest impact is in human relationship. The native is very cautious about revealing too much of oneself and guards the secrets very well. He is very possessive. The native is artistic and creative and has intellectual talents. A Cancer-born individual is generally loyal, hard working and is not afraid of menial tasks. Such people possess an instinct for business combined with imagination that is quite magical for acquiring financial security. The native never gets enough love and approval for he always needs more. (8: p. 68)

Important Cancer occupations would be hotelier, caterer, business executive, accountant, financial adviser, welfare officer, sailor, antique collector, real estate agent, teacher, jeweller, and waitress. A Cancer-born native is protective, emotional, imaginative, moody, loving, creative, artistically gifted, most challenging to get to know and learn, overtly hard but internally cool and reserved, highly emotional and sensitive, greatly compassionate, intuitive, protective of the family and home, makes a loyal parent, abides by the rules to a great extent and loves justice.

## LEO *(Simha)*
August 14—September 13-14

## Main Attributes

A Leo-born native's qualities are excitement, liveliness and high spirits. The native is devoted to the self. Most Leos possess a kingdom, whether small or big, but he is the ruler of it. He is self-assured and often assumes control of a situation. By nature, a Leo individual is showy and expensive. He dislikes the ordinary and the dull. When there is less excitement, he would try to create it. The public image is very important for such a native. He is the most plentiful spender among all the people of the zodiac. If approached in the right way he is the best friend. Such a native is highly egoistic who demands more adoration than respect. At times a Leo individual is also lazy and indolent. (18: p. 26-27)

As Leo is a fixed sign, so such an individual is often determined, stubborn, habit-bound but very confident to lead. The native is often generous, commanding and ambitious, but he is also intolerant, demanding and self-righteous. As his memories are short, he is quick to forgive. A Leo person is often bossy, expensive, generous, loving, impressive, natural leader, greatly enthusiastic, generous and lives life to its fullest. He is often magnificently affectionate, dramatic and creative. He dislikes small-mindedness and meanness but is very dogmatic, often autocratic, unbending but forgiving too. He is fun-loving, sportsman, runner, loves aerobics, polo player, wrestler, weight-lifter, *yoga* lover, football-player. The occupations that a Leo person may love to follow are acting, modelling, fashion designing, company executive, directing films, fire fighting, animal training, and may become a police official. (6: p. 30)

## VIRGO *(Kanya)*
September 15—October 13

# Main Attributes

Both Gemini and Virgo are ruled by the planet Mercury. It inspires its native towards constant activity and drives him to accomplish and be perfect. The native will not postpone any work for tomorrow and will like to finish it today if possible. Such a subject is organised, is not a day-dreamer but a day-doer. Such a native possesses a great capacity for love but love is not enough for him to be happy. The Virgo subject is ambitious, but not just for money. He is very intelligent, possesses excellent memory, analytical mind, and known for clear thinking. The native can look into human minds and has the ability to probe into human motives. People like to consult such a subject for various problems and take advice before putting their plans into action. Such subjects don't like vague ideas. As Virgo is a changeable sign so the native can adjust easily to the change, and new situations. A Virgo individual's nature is shy and reserved. He often prefers small company to converse with, as at such occasions he can offer the best in him. A warm and loving relationship may bring out the best in such a subject because basically he is kind and loyal.

In brief, a Virgo is modest, analytical, critical, painstaking, fussy, intelligent, sharp, foresighted, judicious, hard working, worrying, small-minded, practical to a great extent, restless, diligent, capable, warm and loving, quick thinking, possesses excess mental energy, subject to tension and stress and desires for perfection. Such a native is quite persuasive in communication, always keen to win arguments, and also represents innocence with justice. A Virgo often loves to choose occupations of a secretary, filing clerk, nurse, welfare officer, architect, estimator, banker, accountant, domestic help, writer, computer operator, nutritionist, therapist, teacher, philosopher and legal adviser. (6: p. 34)

## LIBRA *(Tula)*

October 14—November 13

## Main Attributes

A Libra subject is a social person who likes to share his experiences with others. He is quick to form partnerships and friendships, is friendly, popular, attractive, and likes to talk about his high principles and lofty ideals. A Libra native is always happy in finding balance in other things, not merely in human relationships. As a Libra is highly romantic, he is always in search of an ideal mate. A Libra subject is easy to be liked for he possesses a captivating charm and is usually beautiful to look at. Flowers, jewellery and lovely surroundings are the objects of a Libra person's life. The native is at his best in personal relationships. As a Libra person is born under the sign of Scales, he strives for balance and harmony and is happiest when the surrounding environment is serene. A Libran is often a born diplomat. A Libran is affectionate, sentimental, optimistic, and tries hard to please others. However, underneath a friendly exterior, a Libran always longs for love and approval.

A Libran is sociable, diplomatic, angry and aggrieved, charming, easygoing, polite, well-balanced, refined, cool, romantic, impractical, self-seeking, well-read, warm-hearted, out-going, concerned with achieving balance and peace. He loves justice around, easy communication, and is clever, persuasive and frank to a considerable extent. A Libra individual is artistic in nature, music lover and reconciling. Libra occupations are: florist, librarian, fashion designer, publisher, journalist, artist, air steward, musician, hair-dresser, beauty consultant, judge, lawyer, counsellor, media person, actor, secretary, clerk, and sometimes accountant. (6: p. 38)

### SCORPIO *(Vrishchika)*
November 14—December 13-14

## Main Attributes

A Scorpio person is considered to possess extremes. He is identified as powerful, weak, independent, passionate, cold and a bundle of contradictions consisting the best and the worst in human nature. A Scorpio subject would never like to act half-heartedly. He may look calm and smiling at the surface, but is extremely strong willed and determined inside. At times the native is also flexible when solutions are worked out, but if failed in any adventure, he would not accept defeat easily. The subject is extremely agile and never forgets an act of kindness and tries to repay it profusely. He also does not forgive an injury and may wait for years to repay it. A Scorpio subject is most clever with money and likes to amass wealth as spending is not liked by him.

A Scorpio individual is magnetic, passionate, intense, intuitive, possessive, shrewd, determined, jealous, sexually infatuated, intensively private, a great achiever. He possesses ability to overcome challenging situations. He values his intimate relationships and friendships, works hard to exploit the best in those he adores, is easily hurt and responds adversely at times, scientific in outlook, loves to finish the game he is involved in. A Scorpio person likes occupations such as a stockbroker, private detective, police officer, gynaecologist, surgeon, midwife, company director, army officer, psychiatrist, lifeguard, architect, actor, and a farmer. (6: p. 42)

### SAGITTARIUS *(Dhanu)*
December 14—January 13

## Main Attributes

Jupiter rules the sign Sagittarius, so the native is full of life. It is believed a Sagittarius person has the gift from providence. Luck therefore always protects him in friendship, love, marriage, career and money. The native is mostly cheerful. A Sagittarius native is full of enthusiasm, restlessness and joviality and is very progressive. He is adventurous, and loves constant change of scene. The native's restless, inquiring nature requires travel, excitement and to get what is unconventional or untraditional. A Sagittarius individual is always in search for wisdom and tends to be an explorer who loves philosophical pursuits. Such a native is a good friend, is open-hearted, kind, jovial, totally free of malice and ready to help others.

The native loves freedom most and a passion for liberty underlies all other qualities. The native possesses a great sense of humour, and a wide range of interests such as music, nature, philosophy, computer technology, theatre. He is versatile, imaginative, and ready to accept what is untraditional. Briefly, a Sagittarius person is outspoken, optimistic, philosophical, intellectual, freedom-seeking, inconstant, challenge-loving, humorous, possesses boundless energy, explorative, tactless, adventurous, versatile in nature, combines wisdom and bravery, affectionate, extrovert, kind, implicit with knowledge, loves sports such as archery, horse riding, hockey, shooting, football, baseball, etc. (6: p. 46-48)

### CAPRICORN *(Makar)*
January 14—February 13

## Main Attributes

Capricorns are mostly ambitious and spend their lives in the purposeful pursuit of destiny. They strongly desire success, money, status, authority, position and love. The native's personality is implicit with practicality and initiative geared towards attaining leadership and power. Like the Capricorn symbol Goat, the native always tries hard to reach the top. Such a native possesses a great sense of the value of time, which inspires him to become a great organiser and planner. The subject has a great sense of responsibility, discipline and restriction. The native is ambitious, determined, highly diligent, creative, and has no time for idle pursuits. Such a native is often misunderstood by others for he looks cold, and because of his sober nature. The subject is certainly cautious, conservative with money, doesn't like ambiguity and tends to see things clearly. To others the native may appear aloof, indifferent and hard to reach because he is often so self-contained, but his loyalty and affections run deep. He protects those whom he loves.

Briefly, a Capricorn individual is ambitious, prudent, practical, calculative, disciplined, possesses two distinct natures—one is hard working, enterprising, highly motivated and sets high goals of life; the other side is to be lost in an imagined world. At times he cannot find enough motivation to take action and becomes introvert in nature. He loves to work as a judge, lawyer, high-ranking police officer, prison officer, bank executive, engineer, sales executive, secretary, auto mechanic, shopkeeper, teacher, actor, cultivator and a military officer. (6: p. 50)

## AQUARIUS *(Kumbha)*
February 14—March 13

## Main Attributes

An Aquarius individual is either at times an eccentric or a crazy inventor. Like the Water Bearer's fixed sign, the native represents persistent development of the intellect through communication and planetary influence. An Aquarian is often progressive and open-minded but is mostly fixed in his opinion. The native is idealistic, inventive and original and may look easily aloof, detached or even cranky. But the native has a human connection and does not care for the human divisions created by humans. He believes in "I love humankind. It's people I can't stand."

The native possesses intellectual independence and excels in professions in which creativity is needed. His creativity is not limited to just the arts, but can extend to scientific innovations as well as inventions, public service and civil rights reforms, etc. The native has a good chance to work in the media. One can count on him having/creating solutions to problems others thought insoluble. (4: p. 102-103) An Aquarian likes to choose a job as a pilot, airport-worker, electricity worker and electric engineer, scientist, astronomer, astrologer, brain surgeon, psychiatrist, computer operator, entertainer, gynaecologist, film director and actor. (6: p. 35) As he is a visionary, astrologers are found to be born under this sign. Uranus (traditionally Saturn) being the owner of the sign, creates a personality which is liberal, progressive and also fixed in opinion. The native enjoys being with the people but happy to be alone. He loves travelling but feels relaxed to be at home. The subject loves freedom of opinion and to stay free in thinking. (18: p. 55-56)

Briefly, an Aquarian is humane, independent, detached, original, honest, inventive, fiercely individualistic, intellectual and rarely forms permanent relationship with anyone. He is cool, aloof, noted to be friendly, kind, helpful, caring, and possesses deep humanitarian instincts. Essentially, he is a typically private person, possessing originality, creativity and gifted with inventiveness. (10: p. 65)

## PISCES *(Meena)*

March 14—April 13

# Main Attributes

Most Western astrologers reckon that the sign Pisces represents eternity, reincarnation and spiritual rebirth. Pisceans seems to possess other-worldly qualities—mystically being described as possessing half-body and half-spirit. Thus, he is pulled between material and spiritual existence. The native possesses the insight and intuitive powers with which he is able to see deeply into the human psyche. Such natives have extreme sympathy for people who are hurt, animals that are hungry and plants that are sick. At times such a subject is lazy, careless and emotionally confused. Therefore, the native needs to develop a positive self-image and ability to take responsibility. As a Pisces person is blended with compassion and understanding, he exerts a unique power on people whose lives are greatly connected with him. The native may feel lack of confidence as a leader, but he is certainly a guide, teacher and a role model to many.

Briefly, such a native is rich in imagination, intuitive, sensitive, vague, dual-natured, compassionate, easily persuaded, sensual, emotional, dreamer, and a poet. A Piscean is often divided into two extremes—one, wanting to do something real and valuable in the world and the other, moody, self-sacrificing, confused, dependent, retiring to his private world of imagination and dreams. Because of his dual nature he is often prone to extreme nervous tension. Except certain inabilities, he is one of the finest human beings who is a good artist and also a great humanitarian.

A Piscean loves professions of a musician, artist, poet, pharmacist, service engineer, coastguard, fisherman, plumber, oil-rig worker, sailor, nurse, social worker, chemist, counsellor, teacher, soothsayer, forecaster, and even an astrologer (6: p. 58). A Piscean subject loves sports, adores people who love surfing, plays football, ice-skating, water rafting, gymnastics, swimming and cricket.

**The above characteristics must not be seen in isolation to the influences of the other planets in a chart, especially the aspects of beneficial and malefic planets on the ascendant and the owner of the ascendant. Besides, the rising sign in a chart should also be considered to assess the characteristics of an individual. The reader will easily understand the above explanations when he/she goes through the analysis of different charts given in the book. Kindly keep in mind that though the Sun certainly bestows on the individual the characteristics of a sign it transits each month, the aspects of the planets on the ascendant and the rising sign are also important to assess such characteristics finally.**

# The Houses

### The First House

This is the most important house of the horoscope. This is the house of self, the place where the ascendant, personality and self-image resides. It contains the rising sign (*lagna*) and expresses one's personality, temperament, physical health, overall well being, physical characteristics and general attitude towards life. It represents your personal style, mannerism, your likes and dislikes and provides the key to why you look the way you do. It also includes your early childhood and is closely knitted to your health. If successfully deciphered, the first house shows a sense of control and direction. It is so obvious that the focus of this house is going to be your identity. *When a planet transits the ascendant in its own sign it will provide benefits according to the nature of the planet rising in a sign. We have already discussed at length the placements of various planets at the ascendant. The reader needs to keep in mind that the planet occupying the ascendant will surely provide benefits to the native in the light of the strength and characteristics it possesses.*

## The Second House

The second house reveals one's attitude about possessions, security and partners. It is the house where one will find not only one's money and what one owns but what one will own and value, including one's income and those things that one will come to treasure. It also reveals how one feels about one's possessions and will show the best ways how one will earn one's living. It has also to do with one's speech, one's style of conversation, such as aggressive or polite, and family and friendly ties. This house also represents individual's self-esteem, earning abilities and personal resources, making this the house of productivity. Any ruler of ascendant occupying the second house will provide benefits in view of the characteristics the second house contains, as well as the nature of the ascendant. For example, if the owner of the ascendant is Venus and it sits in the second house, it will bestow financial benefits on the native associated with art, acting and culture-related activities; besides, his/her speech will be mild and full of sweet words. *Therefore, the reader needs to remember that the owner of the ascendant when transits in a house other than the ascendant it will bestow qualities, benefits or even losses in view of the characteristics of the house it sits in as well as the qualities the rising sign possesses at the ascendant.*

## The Third House

The third house is concerned with all the nearest relatives, brothers, sisters, friends, cousins etc, but not parents. This house is additionally concerned with communication, (Gemini) transportation and environment. For example, if one is planning to move, the third house may offer advice about what type of environment would be best for the individual—town or country, etc. (10: p. 110) It is also concerned with one's capacity for information-gathering and sharing, and includes one's knowledge, short journeys and immediate environment. Traditionally, this house is also concerned with one's efforts towards life's goals.

## The Fourth House

The fourth house, in fact, is one's home, the place where a house is a home. In addition to being one's domestic life, it is a place where one can feel to be at home with one's unconscious patterns, habits and emotional underpinnings. It is the house where one's foundations of life are seated. The house is related to one's insecurities or need for emotional security. The natural fourth house is ruled by Cancer, so it is associated with the Moon. Thus, the fourth house is both, one's seclusion and self-protection—the place where one can retreat to and depend on. It also indicates the point of one's beginning. As it is related with the Moon, traditionally it is also related with the native's mother and movable as well as immovable property, happiness received from home, vehicles that one would own and, in general, it is also concerned with one's peace and serenity in life. To some extent this house also indicates the direction and place or town where one is likely to settle down. This direction can be reckoned from one's place of birth or parental home. Some Western astrologers consider that the fourth house reflects relationships and connections with one's father as well as father's status.

## The Fifth House

Traditionally, the fifth house is the house of creativity. Thus, naturally, it is related with children, risk-taking, romance and every kind of creative endeavours such as writing, publishing, and investments for productivity. One's creativity is not limited to the arts but one could be creative in any field and direction. The sign occupied by this house indicates the nature of one's creativity and self-expression and its ruler indicates how and where one would develop one's abilities to express oneself. The fifth house also has a strong association with pleasure, particularly one's attitude towards love affairs, the act of love (having children) and the ways one translates emotional and spiritual love into physical. Traditionally, Indian astrologers associate this house mainly with children and education, hence with one's productivity and creativity in any form.

## The Sixth House

The sixth house is related to health but not with physical health like the first house. The sixth house is strongly associated with hygiene and diet, and bowels—all may not be linked to one's physical being. This house also indicates how one handles everyday work and routine whether in business or raising a family. It indicates how disciplined one is when faced with daily routine. This house also reveals (according to the Western tradition) one's attitude towards servants and how one treats those who help in running one's life smoothly. (10: p.111) Indian tradition reveals that this house is associated with litigation, partnership in business, enmity, position of and relationship with the maternal uncle, and communicative qualities.

## The Seventh House

The seventh house mainly highlights the native's attitudes and feelings about emotional relationships or partnerships. In particular, the seventh house reveals one's deep-rooted needs in the area of love, what sort of partner one looks for and how easy or difficult it would be for the individual to maintain harmony in a partnership. The seventh house should always be interpreted together with the fifth house, which indicates one's attitudes towards the act of love and having children. (10: p.111) Western tradition, like the Indian tradition, also considers this house as the house of partnership and marriage. It is associated naturally with the sign Libra that is ruled by Venus. It indicates what kind of partner and marriage one will have. But it indicates other kinds of partnerships as well, such as important friends and associates, business partners, legal affairs and agreements. Above all, one's seventh house indicates where one cooperates and shares with others. (4: p. 220) Indian tradition indicates that this house has to deal primarily with one's marriage, short journeys and at times vocation as well.

## The Eighth House

The eighth house is related with one's shared resources and that includes everything—from taxes, insurance and business mergers to inheritances and marrying for money. It is also known as the house of death and regeneration because it is related to transformation and physical death and deals with transforming physical things into energy. Regeneration is about more than death, too. It is also about individual transformation, whether emotional, physical, mental, or spiritual. It is because of this that this house includes the life forces that are related with sex, birth, and the 'life after life' and death as well. This house also deals with psychic powers, occult mysteries and occult knowledge. (4: p. 223-4) It is strongly associated with endowments and big lottery wins. Crime research and investigations are also highlighted with this. Traditionally (Western) this house is associated with the primal 'life force,' and as such it is inevitably related with sex, and with individual's deepest and most fundamental sexual urges, rather than simple lovemaking. (10: p.112) Indian tradition indicates that this house primarily deals with individual's death and at times sudden gains through lottery or inheritance.

## The Ninth House

It is one of the very important houses besides the ascendant in a chart (*kundali*). The Western system suggests that the ninth house is everything, from higher education to philosophy and religion, from law to long travels and foreign concerns. It also includes politics and all areas of collective thought structures. It is also involved with the development of a social conscience. It is the house of one's social areas, mental exploration, long-distance travels and long journeys overseas, love for seeing new cultures and to know more of the world to gain a new perspective of the world in general. The ninth house is also related to one's efforts in finding new patterns of behaviour and how to break or change them, mainly because of conditioning, beliefs, religion and philosophical systems that are behind all of us. If one takes advantage of this house when its owner is well placed, one can make miracles. It is also the house that relates to publishing and teaching and to convey one's ideas and beliefs openly. As it is naturally associated with the sign Sagittarius, it is the house of exploration and higher mind, mainly of philosophical subjects (4: p. 229) and (10: p. 112). Thus, besides the ascendant, the ninth house is another very important house which describes one's beliefs, likings and leanings, and life's philosophies. It is the ruler of ninth house that describes where and in what manner an individual will involve one's mind and develop understanding of life. Indian tradition considers this house of luck and long distance overseas journeys as well as every kind of religious and spiritual activity that an individual tends to do.

## The Tenth House

It is the house that is related to hope, progress and responsibility. It reveals how well one is getting on in the world—not only financially but in terms of fulfilling one's deepest aspirations, dealing with responsibility and authority, traditional values and social status. It is the house that indicates about one's profession and substantial increase in one's social status. It is the house of one's reputation and career. It is the house where one can find everything outside the home—community standing, social role and what others think of about the individual. Some consider this as the house of ambition, aspiration, and attainment. This house is also related to one of the dominant parents—preferably father. It is the house that indicates success through one's own efforts and a reflection of one's image and achievements. According to the Indian traditions, the tenth house is related to one's *karma* (actions) and profession. It is also the house that reflects the native's father's profession and social status. The sign that rises in this house indicates the subject's profession, life's achievements and also the amount of leaning towards religious activities.

## The Eleventh House

Western astrologers reckon that the eleventh house reveals how one relates to other people socially and is much concerned with friendship and society. This house strongly emphasises how the native would like to engage with the world. It reveals the native's attitude towards political and social opposition, and intolerance. It also indicates how much time the native would give to charitable and humanitarian causes and how he/she works with others, especially in large groups. It also indicates whether the individual would possess genuine affinity for public office! Indian traditions identify this house with the native's personal income, gains through relatives, parents, sudden gains through unknown and undisclosed means, gains through excellent business, general affluence and prosperity. In fact, it is the house which indicates how much wealthy the native should be in his life and how much social status he/she will gather through the riches. A well placed owner of the eleventh house in a chart indicates that the native will surely lead a wealthy and prosperous life.

## The Twelfth House

Western astrologers reckon that this house indicates escapism and isolation. It is also related to hospitals, prisons and mental institutions and all such places where one is likely to experience loneliness and seclusion. It is the house of mystery and related to most psychological problems of the native. (10: p.113) Sometimes this house is also called as the house of sorrows, secrets and self-undoing. Twelfth house is certainly the most mystical of the houses. It is the house where one finds one's subconscious, and the unknown after all. Some Western astrologers reckon this house as the house of troubles, but also make it clear that one's consciousness resides there. This house can lead to self-transcendence, moving one beyond the ego and to what is there beyond the self. (4: p. 243) Indian tradition reckons that this house indicates waste, expenses, losses, long and short journeys and *moksha* as well. In fact, if the owner of this house occupies any beneficial sign or is conjunct with a beneficial planet, it is certainly going to mitigate the good effects of that house and the planet as well.

# Different Aspects from Different Positions

Let us now quickly revise some important matters relating to the planets, for that sort of knowledge is absolutely imperative to assess the strength of a house. In this respect we are reproducing two tables that describe planets' ownerships and unfold their exalted and debilitated positions respectively.

### TABLE 1: Signs that Planets Own

| Planets | Signs the Planets Own |
|---------|----------------------|
| Jupiter | Sagittarius & Pisces |
| Venus | Taurus & Libra |
| Mercury | Gemini & Virgo |
| Mars | Aries & Scorpio |
| Moon | Cancer |
| Sun | Leo |
| Saturn | Capricorn & Aquarius |
| Rahu + | Libra |
| Ketu + | Gemini |

+ Rahu and Ketu are shadow planets and enjoy best in the company of the planets they sit or when they occupy friendly signs ruled by Saturn, Venus or Mercury.

## TABLE 2: Planets' Exalted & Debilitated Positions

| Planets | Exalted | Debilitated |
|---------|---------|-------------|
| Jupiter | Cancer | Capricorn |
| Venus | Pisces | Virgo |
| Mercury | Virgo | Pisces |
| Mars | Capricorn | Cancer |
| Moon | Taurus | Scorpio |
| Sun | Aries | Libra |
| Saturn | Libra | Aries |

Besides the above information, we reckon that the reader also needs to know the planets' aspects that have tremendous impact on individual's personality and way of life. Maharishi Parashar believed that unless one's ascendant has any aspects from the beneficial planets, such as Jupiter, Venus, Mercury and Moon, the native cannot be considered as a good, kind and thoughtful person.

What the Maharishi meant by it was that when the ascendant has aspects from the beneficial planets, their positive effects will always guide him/her to do good things in life. Not only will his thinking be positive, he will also act for the good of his own family and other people. Let us, therefore, examine the planets' aspects before finally assessing the strength of an ascendant or any house.

## TABLE 3: Planets' Aspects from their Positions in a Chart

| | | |
|---------|---------|-------------|
| Jupiter | aspects | **fifth, seventh** and **ninth houses** |
| Venus | aspects | **seventh house** |
| Mercury | aspects | **seventh house** |
| Mars | aspects | **fourth, seventh** and **eighth houses** |
| Moon | aspects | **seventh house** |
| Sun | aspects | **seventh house** |
| Saturn | aspects | **third, seventh** and **tenth houses** |
| Rahu | aspects | **seventh house** |
| Ketu | aspects | **seventh house** |

# Retrograding Planets

Most people who try to indulge with astrological matters believe that retrograding planets are always bad and exert negative influence on a native. But planets sometimes retrograde exactly like human beings who also retreat to renew their energy. When a planet retrogrades in your chart, you generally start considering the functions associated with that particular planet. But never try to judge it considering that it will always do bad to you.

Transiting retrograding planets affect every one of us. As the retrograding planet is off on its retreat, the energy from it will feel different. For example, when Mercury retrogrades, there might be a break in communication for you, and it might affect the running of your car or your e-mails, or other communicating agencies might get interrupted or disturbed. When a planet retrogrades, it is closer to the Earth than usual and therefore, its energies are more intense.

A transiting retrograding planet can be seen as a planet re-gathering or revising its energies. Whatever may be the case, the energy of a transiting retrograding planet is not exactly the same that it normally possesses. Sometimes it is interrupted and at other times it is revised. Therefore, when you start predicting matters about a native, you must keep in mind which planets are retrograding at that time.